Margaret Oliphant

Historical Characters of the Reign of Queen Anne

Margaret Oliphant

Historical Characters of the Reign of Queen Anne

ISBN/EAN: 9783337325237

Printed in Europe, USA, Canada, Australia, Japan

Cover: Foto ©Andreas Hilbeck / pixelio.de

More available books at **www.hansebooks.com**

Historical Characters

of the Reign of

Queen Anne

BY

Mrs. M. O. W. OLIPHANT

NEW YORK
THE CENTURY CO.
1894

THE DE VINNE PRESS.

CONTENTS

INDEX OF ILLUSTRATIONS

THE REIGN OF QUEEN ANNE

THE REIGN OF QUEEN ANNE

CHAPTER I

THE PRINCESS ANNE

THE reign of Queen Anne is one of the most illustrious in English history. In literature it has been common to call it the Augustan age. In politics it has all the interest of a transition period, less agitating, but not less important, than the actual era of revolution. In war, it is, with the exception of the great European wars of the beginning of this century, the most glorious for the English arms of any that have elapsed since Henry V. set up his rights of conquest over France. Opinions change as to the advantage of such superiorities; and, still more, as to the glory which is purchased by bloodshed; yet, according to the received nomenclature, and in the language of all the ages, the time of Marlborough cannot be characterized as anything but glorious. A great general, statesmen of eminence, great poets, men of letters of the first distinction — these are points in which this period cannot easily be excelled. It pleases the fancy to step historically from queen to queen, and to find in each a center of national greatness knitting together the loose threads of the great web. "The spacious times of great Elizabeth" bulk larger and more magnificently in history than those of Anne, but the two eras bear a certain balance which is agreeable to the imagination.

1

And we can scarcely help regretting that the great age of Wordsworth and Scott, Byron and Wellington, should not have been deferred long enough to make the reign of Victoria the third noblest period of modern English history. But time has here balked us. This age is not without its own greatness, but it is not the next in national sequence to that of Anne, as Anne's was to that of Elizabeth.

In the reigns of both these queens this country was trembling between two dynasties, scarcely yet removed from the convulsion of great political changes, and feeling that nothing but the life of the sovereign on the throne stood between it and unknown rulers and dangers to come. The deluge, in both cases, was ready to be let loose after the termination of the life of the central personage in the state. And thus the reign of Anne, like that of Elizabeth, was to her contemporaries the only piece of solid ground amid a sea of evil chances. What was to come after was clear to none.

But in the midst of its agitations and all its exuberant life — the wars abroad, the intrigues at home, the secret correspondences, the plots, the breathless hopes and fears — it is half ludicrous, half pathetic, to turn to the harmless figure of Queen Anne in the center of the scene — a fat, placid, middle-aged woman full of infirmities, with little about her of the picturesque yet artificial brightness of her time, and no gleam of reflection to answer to the wit and genius which have made her age illustrious. A monarch has the strangest fate in this respect: as long as she or he lives, the conscious center of everything whose notice elates and elevates the greatest; but as soon as his day is over, a mere image of state visible among his courtiers only as some unthought-of lackey or faded gentleman usher throws from his little literary lantern a ray of passing illumination upon him. The good things of their lives are thus almost counterbalanced by the insignificance of their historical position. Anne was one of the sovereigns who may, without too great a strain of hyperbole, be allowed to have been beloved in her day. She did nothing to repel the popular devotion. She was the best of wives, the most sadly disappointed of childless mothers. She made pecuniary sacrifices to the weal of her kingdom such as few kings or queens have thought of making. And she was a Stuart, Protestant, and safe, combining all the rights of the family with those of orthodoxy and constitutionalism, without even so much offense as lay in a foreign accent. There was indeed nothing foreign about her, a circumstance in her favor which she shared with the other great English queen regnant, who, like her, was English on both sides of the lineage.

All these points made her popular and, it might be permissible to say, beloved. If she had been indifferent to her father's deprivation, she had not at least shocked popular feeling by any immediate triumph in succeeding him, as Mary had done; and her mild Englishism was delightful to the people after grim William with his Dutch accent and likings. But the historians have not been kind to Anne. They have lavished ill names upon her: a stupid woman,— "a very weak woman, always governed blindly by some female favorite,"— nobody has a civil word to say for her. Yet there is a mixture of the amusing and the tragic in the appearance of this passive figure seated on high, presiding over all the great events of the epoch, with her humble feminine history, her long anguish of motherhood, her hopes so often raised and so often shattered, her stifled family feeling, her profound and helpless sense of misfortune.

There is one high light in the picture, however, though but one, and it comes from one of the rarest and highest sentiments of humanity: the passion of friendship, of which women are popularly supposed to be incapable, but which never existed in more complete and disinterested exhibition than in the bosom of this poor queen. It is sad that it should have ended in disloyalty and estrangement; but, curiously enough, it is not the breach of this close union, but the union itself, which has exposed Anne to the censure and contempt of all her biographers and historians. To an impartial mind we think few things can be more interesting than the position of these two female figures in the foreground of English life. Their friendship brought with it no harm to England; no scandal, such as lurks about the antechamber of kings, and which has made the name of a favorite one of the most odious titles of reproach, could attach in any way to such a relationship. And nothing could be better adapted to enhance the dramatic features of the scene than the contrast between the two friends whose union for many years was so intimate and so complete.

Yet her friend was as like to call forth such devotion as ever woman was. Seldom has there been a more brilliant figure in history than that of the great duchess, a woman beloved and hated as few have ever been; holding on one side in absolute devotion to her the greatest hero of the time, and on the other rousing to the height of adoration the mild and obtuse nature of her mistress; keeping her place on no ground but that of her own sense and spirit, amid all intrigues and opposition, for many of the most remarkable years of English history, and defending herself with such fire and eloquence when attacked, that her plea is as interesting and vivid as any controversy of to-day, and it is impossible to read it without taking a side, with more or less vehemence, in the exciting quarrel. Such a woman, standing like a beautiful Ishmael with every man's hand against her, yet fearing no man, and ready to meet every assailant, makes a welcome variety amid the historical scenes which so seldom exhibit anything so living, so imperious, so bold and free. That she has got little mercy and no indul-

ANNE HYDE, DUCHESS OF YORK.

ENGRAVED BY T. JOHNSON, AFTER THE PAINTING BY SIR PETER LELY,
IN POSSESSION OF EARL SPENCER.

gence, that all chivalrous sentiment has been mute in respect to her, and an angry ill-temper takes possession of every historian who names her name, rather adds to the interest than takes from it. Women in history, strangely enough, seem always to import into the chronicle a certain heat of personal feeling unusual and undesirable in that region of calm. Whether it is that the historian is impatient at finding himself arrested by the troublesome personalities of a woman, and that a certain resentment of her intrusion colors his appreciation of her, or that her appearance naturally possesses an individuality which breaks the line, it is difficult to tell; but the calmest chronicler becomes a partizan when he treats of Mary and Elizabeth, and no man can name Sarah of Marlborough without a heat of indignation or scorn, almost ridiculous, as being so long after date.

To us the unfailing vivacity and spirit of the woman, the dauntless stand she makes, her determination not to be overcome, make her appearance always enlivening ; and art could not have designed a more complete contrast than that of the homely figure by her side, with appealing eyes fixed upon her, a little bewildered, not always quick to understand—a woman born for other uses, but exposed all her harmless life to the fierce light that beats upon a throne. For her part, she has no defense to make, no word to say ; let them spend all their jibes upon her, Anne knows no reply. Her slow understanding and want of perception give her a certain composure which in a queen answers very well for dignity ; yet there is something whimsically pathetic, pitiful, incongruous in the fate which has placed her there, which can scarcely fail to soften the heart of the spectators.

The tragedy of Anne's life, unlike that of her friend, had no utterance, and there was nothing romantic in her appearance or surroundings to attract the lovers of the picturesque. Yet in the blank of her humble intellect she discharged not amiss the duties that were so much too great for her; and if she was disloyal to her friend in the end, that betrayal only adds another touch of pathos to the spectacle of helplessness and human weakness.   It is only the favored few of mankind who are wiser and better, not feebler and less noble, as life draws toward its end.

Anne was, like Elizabeth, the daughter of a subject.   Her mother, Anne Hyde, the daughter of the great Clarendon, though naturally subjected to the hot criticism of the moment on account of that virtue which refused anything less from her prince than the position of wife, was not a woman of much individual character, nor did she live long enough to influence much the training of her daughters.   Historians have not hesitated to sneer at the prudence with which this young lady secured herself by marriage, when so many fairer than she were less scrupulous — a reproach which is somewhat unfair, considering what would certainly have been said of her had she not done so.   Curiously enough, her own father, whether in sincerity or pretense, seems at the moment to have been her most severe critic, exculpating himself with unnecessary energy from all participation in the matter, and declaring that if it were true "the king should immediately cause the woman to be sent to the Tower" till Parliament should have time to pass an act cutting off her head.   It would appear, however, from the contemporary narratives of Pepys and Evelyn that he was not so bad as his words, for he seems to have supported and shielded his daughter during the period of uncertainty which preceded the acknowledgment of her marriage, and to have shared in the general satisfaction afterward.   But this great marriage was not of much advantage to her family.   It did not hinder Clarendon's disgrace and banishment, nor were his sons after him anything advantaged by their close relationship to two queens.

The Duchess of York does not seem to have been remarkable in any way. She is said to have governed her husband; and she died a Roman Catholic,—the first of the royal family to lead the way in that fatal particular: but did not live long enough to affect the belief or training of her children.

There was an interval of three years in age between Mary and Anne. The eldest, Mary, was like the Stuarts, with something of their natural grace of manner; the younger was a fair English child, rosy and plump and blooming; in later life they became more like each other. But the chief thing they inherited from their mother was what is called in fine language, "a tendency to embonpoint," with, it is said, a love of good eating, which helped to produce the other peculiarity.

The religious training of the princesses is the first thing we hear of them. They were put under the charge of a most orthodox tutor, Compton, Bishop of London, with much haste and ostentation — their uncle, Charles II., probably feeling with his usual cynicism that the sop of two extra-Protestant princesses would please the people, and that the souls of a couple of girls could not be of much importance one way or another. How they fared in respect to the other features of education is not recorded. Lord Dartmouth, in his notes on Bishop Burnet's history, informs us that King Charles II., struck by the melodious voice of the little Lady Anne, had her trained in elocution by Mrs. Barry, an actress while Colley Cibber adds that she and her sister were instructed by the well-known Mrs. Betterton to take their parts in a little court performance when Anne was but ten and Mary thirteen; but whether these are two accounts of the same incident, or refer to distinct events, seems doubtful.

The residence of the girls was chiefly at Richmond, where they were under the charge of Lady Frances Villiers, who had a number of daughters of her own, one of whom, Elizabeth, went with Mary to Holland, and was, in some respects, her evil genius. We have, unfortunately, no court chronicle to throw any light upon the lively scene at Richmond, where this little bevy of girls grew up together, conning their divinity, whatever other lessons might be neglected; taking the air upon the river in their barges; following the hounds in the colder season, for this robust exercise seems to have been part of their training. When their youthful seclusion was broken by such a great event as the court mask, in which they played their little parts,— Mrs. Blogge, the saintly beauty, John Evelyn's friend, Godolphin's wife, acting the chief character, in a blaze of diamonds,— or that state visit to the city when King Charles in all his glory took the girls, his heirs, with him, no doubt the old withdrawing-rooms and galleries of Richmond rang with the story for weeks after. Princess Mary, her mind perhaps beginning to own a little agitation as to royal suitors, would have other distractions; but as to the Lady Anne, it soon came to be her chief holiday when the young Duchess of York, her stepmother, came from town in her chariot, or by water, in a great gilded barge breasting up the stream, to pay the young ladies a visit. For in the train of that princess was the young maid of honor, a delightful, brilliant *espiègle*, full of spirit and wilfulness, who bore the undistinguished name of Sarah Jennings, and brought with her such life and stir and movement as dispersed the dullness wherever she went.

There is no such love as a young girl's adoration for a beautiful young woman, a little older than herself, whom she can admire and imitate and cling to, and dream of with visionary passion. This was the kind of sentiment with which the little princess regarded the bright and animated creature in her young stepmother's train. Mary of Modena was herself only a few years older than her stepchildren. They were all young together, accustomed to the perpetual gaiety of the court of Charles II., though, let us hope, kept apart from its license, and

JOHN EVELYN.

ENGRAVED BY E. HEINEMANN, AFTER COPPERPLATE BY F. BARTOLOZZI
IN THE BRITISH MUSEUM.

no shadow of fate seems to have fallen upon the group of girls
in their early peaceful days. Anne in particular would seem to
have been left to hang upon the arm and bask in the smiles of
her stepmother's young lady in waiting at her pleasure — with
many a laugh at premature favoritism. "We had used to play
together when she was a child," said the great duchess long
after. "She even then expressed a particular fondness for me;
this inclination increased with our years. I was often at court,
and the princess always distinguished me by the pleasure she
took to honor me preferably to others with her conversation
and confidence. In all her parties for amusement, I was sure
by her choice to be one."

Mistress Sarah was one of the actors in the mask above
referred to; she was in the most intimate circle of the Duke
of York's household, closely linked to all its members, in that
relationship, almost as close as kindred, which binds a court
together.

And no doubt it added greatly to the attractions which
the bright and animated girl exercised over her playmates and
companions, that she had already a romantic love-story, and, at a
period when matches were everywhere arranged, as at present
in continental countries, by the parents, made a secret marriage,
under the most romantic circumstances, with a young hero already a soldier of distinction. He was not an irreproachable
hero. Court scandal had not spared him. He was said to have
founded his fortune upon the bounty of one of the shameless
women of Charles's court. But the imagination of the period
was not over-delicate, and probably had he not become so
great a man, and acquired so many enemies, we should have
heard little of John Churchill's early vices. About his sister,
Arabella Churchill, unfortunately there could not be any doubt;
and it is a curious instance of the sudden efflorescence now
and then of a race which neither before nor after is of particular

note, that Marlborough's sister should have been the mother
of that one illustrious Stuart who might, had he been legitimate, have changed the fortunes of the house — the Duke
of Berwick. Had she, instead of Anne Hyde, been James's
duchess, what a difference might have been made in history! Nobody had heard of the Churchills before — they
have not been a distinguished race since. It is curious that
they should have produced, all unawares, without preparation
or warning, the two greatest soldiers of the age.

Young Churchill was attached to the Duke of York's service,
as Sarah Jennings was to that of the duchess. He had served
abroad with distinction. In 1672, when France and England for
once, in a way, were allies against Holland, he had served under
the great Turenne, who called him "my handsome Englishman,"
and vaunted his gallantry. He was but twenty-two when he
thus gave proofs of his future greatness. When he returned,
after various other exploits, and resumed his court service, the
brilliant maid of honor, whom the little princess adored, attained a complete dominion over the spirit of the young soldier.
There were difficulties about the marriage, for he had no fortune, and his provident parents had secured an heiress for him.
But it was at length accomplished so secretly that even the bride
was never quite certain of the date, in the presence and with the
favor of Mary of Modena herself. Sarah, if the dates are
correct, must have been eighteen at this period, and her little
princess fourteen. What a delightful interruption to the dullness of Richmond to hear all about it when the Duchess of
York came with her train and the two girls could wander
away together in some green avenue till Lady Frances sent
a page or an usher after them!

Mary of Modena must have been a lover of romances, and
true love also, though her youth had fallen to such a gruesome
bridegroom as James Stuart; for not only Sarah Jennings

and her great general, who were to have so great a hand in
keeping that poor lady's son from his kingdom, but Mary
Blogge and her statesman, who was to rule England so wisely
in the interest of the opposing side, were both secretly married
under the young duchess's wing, she helping, planning, and
sanctioning the secret. How many additional bitternesses must
this have put into her cup when she was sitting, a shadow
queen, at St.-Germain, and all those people whom she had
loved and caressed were swaying the fortunes of England!
And who can tell what tender recollections of his secret wedding and the sweet and saintly prude whom King James's
young wife gave him, may have touched the soul of Godolphin
in those hankerings after his old master—if it were not, as
scandal said, to his old mistress—which moved him from time
to time, great minister as he was, almost to the verge of treachery! The Churchills, it must be owned, showed little gratitude
to their royal patrons.

When the Princess Mary married and went to Holland with
her husband, the position of her sister at home became a more
important one. Anne was not without some experience of
travel and those educational advantages which the sight of
foreign countries are said to bring. She went to The Hague
to visit her sister. She accompanied her father, sturdy little
Protestant as she was, when he was in disgrace for his religious
views, and spent some time in Brussels, from which place she
wrote to one of the ladies about the court a letter which has
been preserved,— with just as much and as little reason as any
other letter of a fifteen-year-old girl with her eyes about her, at
a distance of two hundred years,— in which the young lady
describes a ball she had seen, herself *incognita*, at which some
gentlemen "danced extremely well — as well if not better
than the Duke of Monmouth or Sir E. Villiers, which I think
is very extraordinary," says the girl, no doubt sincerely believ-

ing that the best of all things was to be found at home. She
had little difficulties about her spelling, but that was common
enough.   "As for the town," says the Princess Anne, "methinks tho' the streets are not so clean as in Holland, yet they
are not so dirty as ours; they are very well paved and very
easy — they only have od smells."   This is a peculiarity which
has outlived her day, and it would seem to imply that England,
even before the invention of sanitary science, was superior in
this respect at least to the towns of the Continent.

After these unusual dissipations Anne remained in the shade
until she married, in 1683, George, Prince of Denmark, a perfectly inoffensive and insignificant person, to whom she gave,
during the rest of her life, a faithful, humdrum, but unbroken
attachment, such as shows to little advantage in print, but
makes the happiness of many a home.   This marriage was
another sacrifice to the Protestantism of England, and in that
point of view pleased the people much.   King Charles, glad to
satisfy the country by any act which cost him nothing, thought
it "very convenient and suitable."   James, unwilling, but pow-
erless, grumbled to himself that "he had little encouragement
in the conduct of the Prince of Orange to marry another
daughter in the same interest," but made no effort against it.
The prince himself produced no very great impression, one
way or another, as indeed he was little fitted to do.   "He has
the Danish countenance, blonde," says Evelyn, in his diary;
"of few words; spoke French but ill; seemed somewhat heavy,
but is reported to be valiant."   He had never any occasion to
show his valor during his long residence in England, but many
to prove the former quality,—the heaviness,—which was only too
evident; but Anne herself was not brilliant, and she was made
for friendship, not for passion in the ordinary sense of the word.
She never seems to have been in the smallest way dissatisfied
with her heavy, honest goodman.   He was fond of eating and

PRINCE GEORGE OF DENMARK.

ENGRAVED BY R. A. MULLER, FROM MEZZOTINT IN THE BRITISH MUSEUM
BY JOHN SMITH, AFTER THE PAINTING BY SIR GODFREY KNELLER.

drinking, but of no more dangerous pleasures. Her peace of mind was fluttered by no rival, nor her feminine pride touched. Her attendants might be as seductive as they pleased, this steady, stolid husband was immovable, and there is no doubt that the princess appreciated the advantages of this immunity from one of the thorns which were planted in every other royal pillow.

Her marriage had another advantage of giving her a household and court of her own, and enabled her at once to secure for herself the companionship of her always beloved friend. "So desirous was she," says Duchess Sarah, "of having me always near her, that upon her marriage with the Prince of Denmark, in 1683, it was at her own earnest request to her father I was made one of the ladies of her bedchamber. What conduced to make me the more agreeable to her in this station was, doubtless," she adds with candor, "the dislike she conceived to most of the other persons about her, and particularly for her first lady of the bedchamber — the Countess of Clarendon, a lady whose discourse and manner could not possibly recommend her to so young a mistress; for she looked like a mad-woman and talked like a scholar. Indeed, her highness's court was so oddly composed that I think it would be making myself no great compliment if I should say her choosing to spend more of her time with me than with any of her other servants did no discredit to her taste."

Lady Clarendon was the wife of the great chancellor's son, and was thus the aunt, by marriage, of the princess — not always a very endearing relationship. She was not a great lady by birth, and though a friend of Evelyn's and a highly educated woman, might easily be supposed to be a little oppressive in a young household where her relationship gave her a certain authority.

The prince was dull, the princess had not many resources.

They settled down in homely virtue, close to the court with all its scandals and gaieties, but not quite of it; and nothing could be more natural than that Anne should eagerly avail herself of the always amusing, always lively companion who had been the friend of her youth.　The Cockpit, which was Anne's residence, had been built as a royal playhouse, first for the sport indicated by its name, then for the more refined amusements of the theater, but had been afterward turned into a private residence, and bought by Charles II. for his niece on her marriage. It formed part of the old palace of Whitehall, and must have been within sight and sound of the constant gaieties going on in that lawless household, in the best of which the princess and her attendant would have their natural share.　No doubt to hear Lady Churchill's lively satirical remarks upon all this, and the flow of her brilliant malice, must have kept the household lively, and brightened the dull days and tedious waitings of maternity, into which Anne was immediately plunged, drawing a laugh even from stupid George in the chimney-corner.　And there was this peculiarity to make the whole more piquant; that it was virtue, irreproachable, and no doubt pleasantly self-conscious of its superiority, which thus got its fun out of vice.　The two young couples on the other side of the way were immaculate, devoted exclusively to each other, thinking of neither man nor woman save their lawful mates.　Probably neither the princess nor her lady in waiting were disgusted by gossip about the Portsmouths and Castlemaines, but took these ladies to pieces with indignant zest and spared no jibe.　And though the remarks might be too broad for modern liking, and the fun somewhat unsavory, we cannot but think that amidst the noisy and picturesque life of that wild Restoration era, full of corruption, yet so gay and sparkling to the spectator, this little household of the Cockpit is not without its claims upon our attention.　There was not in all Charles's court so splendid a

couple as the young Churchills: he already one of the most
distinguished soldiers of the age, she a beautiful young woman
overflowing with wit and energy.　And Princess Anne was
very young; in full possession of that *beauté de diable* which,
so long as it lasts, has its own charm, the beauty of color and
freshness and youthful contour.　She had a beautiful voice, the
prettiest hands, and the most affectionate heart.　If she were
not clever, that matters but little to a girl of twenty, taught by
love to be receptive, and called upon for no effort of genius.
Honest George behind backs was not much more than a piece
of still life, but an inoffensive and amiable one, taking nothing
upon him.　If there was calculation in the steadfastness with
which the abler pair possessed themselves of the confidence,
and held fast to the service of their royal friends, it would be
hard to assert that there was not some affection too, at least on
the part of Sarah, who had known every thought of her little
princess's heart since she was a child, and could not but be flattered and pleased by the love showered upon her.　At all events,
in Anne there was no unworthy sentiment; everything about her
appeals to our tenderness.　When she attained what seems to
have been the summit of her desires and secured her type of excellence, the admired and adored paragon of her childhood, for
her daily companion, the formal titles and addresses which her
rank made necessary became irksome beyond measure to the
simple-hearted young woman whose hard fate it was to have
been born a princess.　The impetuosity of her affection, her
rush, so to speak, into the arms of her friend, her pretty
youthful sentiment, so fresh and natural, her humility and simplicity, are all pleasant to contemplate.　Little more than a
year after her marriage, after the closer union had begun, she
writes thus:

If you will let me have the satisfaction of hearing from you again
before I see you, let me beg of you not to call me " your highness " at

every word, but to be as free with me as one friend ought to be with another. And you can never give me any greater proof of your friendship than in telling me your mind freely in all things, which I do beg of you to do: and if it ever were in my power to serve you, nobody would be more ready than myself. I am all impatience for Wednesday. Till then farewell.

Upon this there ensued a little sentimental bargain between the two young women. It was not according to the manners of the time that they should call each other Anne and Sarah, and the fashion of the Aramintas and Dorindas had not yet arrived from Paris. They managed the transformation necessary in a curiously matter-of-fact and English way:

She grew uneasy to be treated by me with the form and ceremony due to her rank; nor could she bear from me the sound of words which implied in them distance and superiority. It was this turn of mind which made her one day propose to me that whenever I should happen to be absent from her we might in all our letters write ourselves by feigned names, such as would import nothing of distinction of rank between us. Morley and Freeman were the names her fancy hit upon, and she left me to choose by which of them I should be called. My frank open temper led me naturally to pitch upon Freeman, and so the princess took the other; and from this time Mrs. Morley and Mrs. Freeman began to converse as equals, made so by affection and friendship.

Very likely these were the names in some young lady's book which had been in the princess's childish library,— something a generation before the " Spectator,"— in which rural virtues and the claims of friendship were the chief subjects. Morley is one of the typical names of sentimental literature in the eighteenth century, and might be originally introduced by some precursor of those proper little romances which have in all ages been considered the proper reading for " the fair."

Mrs. Morley could be no other than the gentle *ingénue*, the type of modest virtue, and Freeman was of all others the title most suitable for Sarah, the bright and brave. Historians have not been able to contain themselves for angry ridicule of this

CHARLES II.

ENGRAVED BY T. JOHNSON, AFTER ORIGINAL PAINTING BY SAMUEL COOPER,
IN THE GALLERY OF THE DUKE OF RICHMOND AND GORDON.

little friendly treaty. To us it seems a pretty incident. The princess was twenty, the bedchamber woman twenty-four. Their friendly traffic had not to their own consciousness attained the importance of a historical fact.

The locality in which the royal houses in London stood was very different then from its appearance now. Whitehall at present is a great thoroughfare, full of life and movement, with but one remnant of the old palace,— once the banqueting-hall, now the chapel royal, where the window out of which Charles I. is supposed to have passed to the scaffold is pointed out to strangers,— and still presenting a bit of gloomy, stately front to the street.

St. James's Park opposite is screened off and separated now by the Horse Guards and other public buildings, a long and heavy line which forms one side of the way. But in those days there were neither public buildings nor busy street. The palace, straggling and irregular, with walls and roofs on many different levels, stood like a sort of royal village between the river and the park, with the turrets of St. James twinkling in the distance, in the sunshine, over the trees of the Mall, where King Charles with all his dogs and gentlemen would stream forth daily for his saunter or his game. The Cockpit was one of the outlying portions of Whitehall upon the edge of the park.

Anne had been but two years married when King Charles died. And then the aspect of affairs changed. The mass in the private chapel, and the presence here and there of somebody who looked like a priest, at once started into prominence and began to alarm the gazers more than the dissolute amusements of the court had ever done. James was not virtuous any more than his brother. One of the first acts which the excellent Evelyn, one of the best of men, had to do as commissioner of the privy seal, was to affix that imperial stamp to a patent by

2

which one of the new king's favorites was made Countess of Dor-
chester; but James's immoralities were not his chief characteristics.   He was a more dangerous king than Charles, who was
merely selfish, dissolute, and pleasure-loving.   James was more;
he was a bigoted Roman Catholic, eager to raise his faith to its
old supremacy, and the mere thought that the door which had
been so bolted and barred against popery was now set open
filled all England with the wildest panic.   The nation felt itself
caught by the torrent which must carry it to destruction.   Men
saw the dungeons of the Inquisition, the fires of Smithfield, before them as soon as the proscribed priest was readmitted and
mass once more openly said at an unconcealed altar.   Never
was there a more universal or all-influential sentiment.   The
terror, the unanimity, are things to wonder at.   Sancroft and his
bishops were not constitutionalists.   The personal rule of the
king had nothing in it that alarmed them; but the idea of the
reintroduction of popery awoke such a panic in their bosoms as
drove them, in spite of their own tenets, into resistance; and,
for the first time absolutely unanimous, England was at their
back.   When we take history piecemeal, and read it through
the individual lives of the chief actors, we perceive with the
strangest sensations of surprise that at these great crises not
one of the leaders of the nation was sure what he wanted or
what he feared, or was even entirely sincere in his adherence to
one party against another.   They were the courtiers of James,
and invited William; they were William's ministers, and kept
up a correspondence with James.   The best of them was not
without a treacherous side.   They were never certain which
was safest, which would last; always liable to lend an ear to
temptations from the other party, never sure that they might
not to-morrow morning find themselves in open rebellion against
the master of to-day.   Yet, while almost every individual of
note was subject to this strange uncertainty, this confused

and troubled vacillation, there was such a sweep of national
conviction, so strong a current of the general will, that the
supposed leaders of opinion were carried away by it, and compelled to assume and act upon a conviction which was England's, but which individually they did not possess. Nothing
can be made more remarkable, more unexplainable under any
other interpretations, than the way in which his entire court,
statesmen, soldiers, all who were worth counting, and so many
who were not, abandoned King James — some with a sort of
consternation, not knowing why they did it, driven by a force
they could not resist. No example of this can be more remarkable than that of Clarendon, who received the news of his son's
defection to the Prince of Orange with what seems to be a
heartbroken cry: "O God! that my son should be a rebel!"
yet, presently, ten days afterward, is drawn away himself in a
kind of extraordinary confusion, like a man in a dream, like a
subject of mesmeric influence, although in all the following
negotiations he maintained James's cause as far as a man could
who did not accept ruin as a consequence. Scarcely one of
these men was whole-hearted or had any determined principle
in the matter. But in the mass of the nation behind them
was a force of conviction, of panic, of determination, that carried them off their feet. The chief names of England appear
little more than straws upon the current, indicating its course,
but forced along by its fierce sweep and impetus, and not by
any impulse of their own.

The Princess Anne occupied a very different position from
that of these bewildered statesmen. She had been brought up
in the strictest sect of her religion, Protestant almost more than
Christian, a churchwoman above all. To those who are capable of thinking about their faith it is always possible to believe
in the thoughts of other people, and conceive the likelihood, at
least, that they, in their own esteem, if not in any one else's,

may be right — which is the only true foundation of toleration. But it is the people who believe without thinking, who receive what they are taught without exercising any judgment of their own upon the subject, and cling to it in exactly the same form in which they received it, with a conviction that its least important detail is as necessary as its first principle, who furnish that *sancta simplicitas* which makes the cruelest persecution possible without turning the persecutors into fiends and barbarians. Though her mother had been a Roman Catholic, and her father was one, and though many of her relations belonged to the old church, Anne was a Protestant of the most unyielding kind. She was in herself as good a type of the England of her time as could have been found, far better than her abler and larger-minded advisers. The narrowness of her mind and the rigidity of her faith were above all reassurances of reason, all guarantees of possibility. She was as much dismayed by her father's determination to liberate and tolerate popery as the least enlightened of his subjects. " Methinks it has a very dismal prospect," she wrote as early as 1686, only the year after James's accession. "Attempts," Lady Marlborough tells us, " were made to draw his daughter into his designs. The king, indeed, used no harshness with her; he only discovered his wishes by putting into her hands some books and papers which he hoped might induce her to a change of religion, and had she had any inclination that way the chaplains about were such divines as could have said but little in defense of their own religion or to secure her against the pretenses of Popery recommended to her by a father and a king." This low estimate of the princess's spiritual advisers is whimsically supported by Evelyn's opinion of Anne's first religious preceptor,— Bishop Compton,—of whom the courtly philosopher declared after hearing a sermon from him that "this worthy person's talent is not preaching."

HENRY COMPTON, BISHOP OF LONDON.

But Anne required no persuading to stimulate her in the fear
of popery and narrow devotion to the church, outside of which
she knew of no salvation. No doubt her father's popish tracts,
things which in that age were held to possess many of the prop-
erties of the dynamite of to-day, scared the inflexible and un-
imaginative churchwoman as much as if they had been capable
of exploding and doing her actual damage. Her training, so
wisely adapted to please the Protestant party, had probably been
thought by her father and uncle to be a matter of complete indifference on any other ground; but in this way they reckoned
altogether without their princess. With both James's daughters
the process was too successful. They feared popery more than
they loved their father. There seems not the slightest reason to
suppose that Anne was insincere in her anxiety for the church,
or that the panic which she shared with the whole country was affected or unreal. It is impossible that she could expect her own
position to be improved by the substitution of her sister and her
sister's husband for the father who had always been kind to her.
The Churchills, whose church principles were not perhaps so
undeniable, and whose regard for their own interest was great,
are more difficult to divine; and yet it appears an unnecessary
thing to refer their action to unworthy motives. It is asserted
by some that they had some visionary plan after they had over-
turned the existing economy by the help of William, of bringing in their princess by a side wind and reigning through her
over the startled and subjugated nation. But granting that such
an imagination might have been conceived in the fertile and
restless brain of a young and sanguine woman, it seems impossible to imagine that Churchill — a man of some experience in
the world, and some knowledge of William — could even for a
moment have believed that the grave and ambitious prince, who
was so near the throne, could have been persuaded or forced to
waive his wife's claims, and those still more imperative ones

which his position of Deliverer gave him, in order to advance
the fortunes of any one else, least of all of the sister-in-law
whom he despised.

It is half ludicrous, half pathetic, in the midst of all the tu-
mult and confusion of the time, to note the constant allusions to
the princess's condition, which recurs whenever she is mentioned.   There were always reasons why it should be especially
cruel to disturb her, and her state had constantly to be taken
into account.   It was very natural in such circumstances that
she should more and more cling to her stronger friend, and find
no comfort out of her presence.   " Whatever changes there are
in the world, I hope you will never forsake me, and I shall be
happy," she writes during this period of excitement and distress.
She herself was weak and not very wise.   In a sudden emer-
gency neither she nor her husband were good for much.   They
could carry on the routine of life well enough, but when unfore-
seen necessities came they stood helpless and bewildered ; but
Lady Churchill was quick of wit and full of inexhaustible resource.   To her it was always given to know what to do.

It is unnecessary here to enter into the history of what
is called the Great Revolution.   It is the great modern turning-
point of English history, and no doubt it is one of the reasons
why we have been exempted in later days from the agitations
of desperate and bloody revolutions which have shaken all
neighboring nations.   Glorious and happy, however, scarcely
seem to be fit words to describe this extraordinary event.   A
more painful era does not exist in history.   There is scarcely an
individual in the front of affairs who was not guilty of treachery
at one time or another.   They betrayed one another on every
hand ; they were perplexed, uncertain, full of continual alarms.
The king who went away was a gloomy bigot; the king who
came was a cold and melancholy alien.   Enthusiasm there was
none, nor even conviction, except of the necessity of doing some-

thing of a wide-reaching and undeniable change. The part
which the ladies at the Cockpit played brings the hurry and excitement of the movement to its crisis. Both in their way were
anxious for their respective husbands, absent in the suite of
James, and still in his power. When the report came that Lord
Feversham had begged of James "on his knees two hours " to order the arrest of Churchill, Mrs. Freeman must have needed all
her courage; while the faithful Morley wept, yet tried to emulate the braver woman, wondering in her excitement what her
own heavy prince was doing, and eager for William's advance,
which, somehow or other, was to bring peace and quiet. That
heavy prince meanwhile was mooning about with the perplexed
and unhappy king, uttering out of his blond mustache with an
atrocious accent his dull wonder, "Est il possible?" as every
new desertion was announced, till mounting heavily one evening
after dinner, warmed and encouraged by a good deal of King
James's wine, and riding through the cold and dark, in his turn
he deserted too. When this event happened, the excitement at
the Cockpit was overwhelming. The princess was "in a great
fright." "She sent for me," says Lady Churchill, " told me her
distress, and declared that rather than see her father, she would
jump out of window." King James was coming back to London, sad and wroth, and perhaps the rumor that he would
have her arrested lent additional terrors to the idea of encoun-
tering his angry countenance. Lady Churchill went immediately to Bishop Compton, the princess's early tutor and confidential adviser, and instant means were taken to secure her
flight. That very night, after her attendants were in bed, Anne
rose in the dark, and with her beloved Sarah's arm and support
stole down the back stairs to where the bishop, in a hackney
coach, was waiting for her. Other princesses in similar situations have owned to a thrill of pleasure in such an adventure.
No doubt at least she breathed the freer when she was out of

the palace where King James with his dark countenance might have come any day to demand from her an account of her husband's behavior, or to upbraid her with her own want of affection. Anyhow, the sweep of the current had now reached her tremulous feet, and she had no power any more than stronger persons of resisting it.

Anne's position was very much changed by the Revolution. If any ambitious hopes had been entertained or plans formed by her household, they were speedily and very completely brought to an end. The dull royal pair with their two brilliant guides and counselors now found themselves confronted by another couple of very different mark: the serious, somewhat gloomy, determined, and self-concentrated Dutchman, and the new queen, Mary, a person far more attractive and imposing than Anne; two people full of character and power. We have no space here, however, to appropriate to these remarkable persons. William, in particular, belongs to larger annals and a history more important than these sketches. Mary has left an epitome of herself in her letters which is among the most wonderful of individual revelations; but this cannot now be our theme, though the subject is a most attractive one.

Two persons so remarkable threw into the shade even Churchill and Sarah, much more good Anne and George. We have no reason to suppose that Mary entertained any particular sentiment whatever toward her sister, from whom she had been entirely separated for the greater part of her life, and the history of their relations is a painful one from beginning to end. No doubt the queen regarded the household of the princess with the contempt which a woman with so entirely different a code would naturally entertain for a family in which the heads were so lax and secondary, the counselors so prominent. There was nothing in Mary which would help her to understand the feeling with which Anne regarded her friend

JAMES II. IN HIS CORONATION ROBES.

Mary. She had herself made use of their influence in the time
when it was all important to secure every power in England
for William's service, but a proud distaste for the woman whom
the princess trusted as her equal soon awoke in the bosom of the
queen. The Churchills, however, served the new sovereigns
signally by persuading the princess to yield her own rights, and
consent to the conjoint reign, and to William's life sovereignty —
no small concession on the part of the next heir, and one which
only the passive character of Anne could have made to appear
insignificant.

Had she been a stronger and more intellectual woman, this
act would have borne the aspect of a magnanimous and noble
sacrifice to the good of the country, of her own interests, and
that of her children. As it was, her self-renunciation has got
her very little credit, either then or now, and it has been considered rather an evidence of the discretion of the Churchills
than of the generosity and patriotism of the princess. These,
perhaps, are rather large words to use in speaking of Anne,
but it must be remembered that a narrow mind is usually not
less, but more, tenacious of personal honor and advantage than
a great one, and that the dimmer an understanding may be, the
less it is accessible to high reason and noble motive. This
sacrifice accomplished, however, there commenced a petty war
between Whitehall and the Cockpit, in which perhaps Mary
and Lady Churchill (now Marlborough) were the chief comba-
tants, but which from henceforward until her sister's death became the principal feature in Anne's life. Continued squabbling
is never lovely even when it is between queens and princesses,
but in this case the injured person has had no little injustice,
and the offender so many partizans that it may not be amiss to
make Anne's side of the question a little more apparent.

If her friend was to blame for embroiling Anne with the
queen, it can scarcely be believed that the princess's case would

have been more satisfactory had she been left in her helplessness to the tender mercies of William, and entirely dependent upon his kindness, which must have happened had there been no bold and strong adviser in the matter. There was no generosity in the treatment which Anne received from the royal pair. She had made a sacrifice to the security of their throne which deserved some grace in return. But her innocent fancy for the palace at Richmond, where the sisters had been brought up together, was not indulged, nor would there be much excuse even if she were in the wrong for the squabblings about her lodging at Whitehall. But she cannot be said to have been in the wrong in the next question which occurred, which was the settlement of her own income. This she had previously drawn from her father, according to the existing custom in the royal family, and James had been always liberal and kind to her. But it was a different thing to depend upon the somewhat grudging hand of an economical brother-in-law, who had a number of foreign dependents to provide for, and a great deal to do with the money granted to him. He alarmed her friends on this point at once by a remark made to Clarendon as to what the princess could want with so large an income as thirty thousand a year; and he does not seem at any time or in any particular to have shown consideration for her. Perhaps the Churchills were afraid that their mistress would be less able than usual to help and further their own fortunes, as is universally alleged against them; but, had they been the most disinterested couple in the world, it would still have been their duty to do what they could to secure her against any caprice of the new king, who had no right to be the arbiter of her fate. Lady Marlborough's strenuous action to bring the question to the decision of Parliament was nothing less than her mistress's interests demanded. And the sense of the country was so far with them that the princess's income was settled with very little difficulty upon a more liberal basis than her father's allowance; which, considering that she, and the children of whom she was every year becoming the mother, were the only acknowledged heirs of the throne, was a perfectly natural and just arrangement.

But the king and queen did not see it in this light. "Friends! what friends have you but the king and me?" Queen Mary asked with indignation. It is not to be supposed that she meant any harm to her sister, but with also a sufficiently natural sentiment could not see what Anne's objection was to dependence upon herself.

The position on both sides is so clearly comprehensible that the strength of party feeling which makes Lord Macaulay defend the somewhat petty attitude of his favorite monarch on the occasion is very extraordinary. It requires no very subtle penetration to see the difference between an allowance that comes from a father and that which depends upon the doubtful friendship of a brother-in-law. Anne had fully proved her capacity to consider the public weal above her own, and it was unworthy of William even to wish to keep in the position of a hanger-on a woman who had so greatly promoted the harmony of his own settlement.

Parliament finally voted her a revenue of fifty thousand pounds a year, as a sort of compromise between the thirty thousand pounds which King William grudged her and the unreasonably large sum which some of her supporters hoped to obtain; but the king and queen never forgave her, and still less her advisers, for what they chose to consider a want of confidence in themselves.

But William was always impatient of the incapable, and the permission was absolutely denied to him. In all these claims and refusals the position of Lady Marlborough as the princess's right hand had been completely acknowledged by Queen Mary and her husband, who indeed attempted secret negotiations with her on more than one occasion to induce her to moderate Anne's claims and to persuade her into compliance with their wishes. "She [the queen] sent a great lord to me to desire I would persuade the Princess to keep the Prince from going to sea; and this I was to compass without letting the Princess know it was the Queen's desire . . . after this the Queen sent Lord Rochester to me to desire much the same thing. The Prince was not to go to sea, and this not going was to appear his own choice."

Similar attempts were made in the matter of the allowance. And it is scarcely possible to believe that Mary, a queen who was not without some of the absolutism of the Stuart mind, should have failed to feel a certain exasperation with the bold woman who thus upheld her sister's little separate court and interest, and was neither to be flattered nor frightened into subservience. And very likely this little separate court was a thorn in the side of the royal pair, keeping constant watch upon all their actions, maintaining a perpetual criticism, no doubt leveling many a jibe at the Dutch retainers, and still more at the Dutch master. Good-natured friends, even in the capacity of courtiers, were no doubt found to whisper in the presence-chamber the witticisms with which Sarah of Marlborough would entertain her mistress — utterances not very brilliant, perhaps, but sharp enough. It would not sweeten the temper of the queen if she found out, for instance, that her great William was known as Caliban in the correspondence of Mrs. Morley and Mrs. Freeman. A hundred petty irritations always come in in such circumstances to increase a breach. What the precise occurrence was which brought about the final explosion is not known, but one day after a stormy scene, in which the queen had in vain demanded from her sister the dismissal of Lady Marlborough, an event occurred which took away everybody's breath.

MARY, PRINCESS OF ORANGE.

This was the sudden dismissal, without reason assigned, at least so far as the public knew, of Lord Marlborough from all his offices. He was lieutenant-general of the army, and he was a gentleman of the king's bedchamber. Up to this time there had been nothing to find fault with in his conduct. William was too good a soldier himself not to appreciate Marlborough's military talents, and he had behaved, if not with any enthusiasm for the new order of affairs, with good taste at least in very difficult circumstances. His desertion of James and his powerful presence and influence on the opposite side had contributed much to the bloodless victory of the' Prince of Orange; but except so far as this went, Marlborough had shown no hostility to his old master. In the convention he had voted for a regency, and when it became evident that William's terms must be accepted unconditionally or not at all, he had refrained from voting altogether; so that his support might be considered lukewarm. But, on the other hand, he had served with great distinction abroad, acting with perfect loyalty to his new chief while in command of the English forces. In short, his public aspect up to this time would seem on the face of it to have been irreproachable.

This being the case, his sudden dismissal from court filled his friends with astonishment and dismay. Nobody understood its why or wherefore. " An incident happened which I unwillingly mention," says Bishop Burnet, "because it cannot be told without some reflection on the memory of the queen, whom I always honored beyond all the persons whom I have ever known." This regretful preface affords an excellent guarantee of the bishop's sincerity; but Lord Macaulay omits his statement of the case altogether while quoting passages from the then unpublished manuscript which seemed to support his own views. "The Earl of Nottingham," Burnet continues, "came to the Earl of Marlborough with a message from the King telling him that he had no more use for his services, and therefore he demanded all his commissions. What drew so sudden and hard a message was not known, for he had been with the King that morning and had parted with him in the ordinary manner. It seemed some letter was intercepted that gave suspicions : it is certain that he thought he was too little considered, and that he had upon many occasions censured the King's conduct and reflected on the Dutch." Lord Macaulay, on the other hand, ignoring this statement, assures his readers that the real ground of the dismissal had been communicated to Anne on the previous night (notwithstanding that the great general had been privileged to put on the king's shirt next morning as if nothing had happened), and that it was in reality the discovery of a plot for James's restoration, conceived by Marlborough, and in which the princess herself was implicated. It was reported to be Marlborough's intention to move in the House of Lords an address to William, requesting him to dismiss the foreign servants who surrounded him, and of whom the English were bitterly jealous. Such a scheme of reprisals would have had a certain humor in its summary reversal of the position, and no doubt must Sarah herself have had some hand in its construction, if it ever existed. William was as little likely to give up Bentinck and Keppel as Anne was to sacrifice the friends whom she loved, and a breach between the Parliament and the king would have been, it was hoped, the natural result —to be followed by a *coup d'état*, in which James might be replaced under stringent conditions upon the throne. The sole evidence for this plot is King James himself, who describes it in his diary. Lord Macaulay adds that it is strongly confirmed by Burnet, but this, we take leave to think, is not the case. At the same time there seems no reason to doubt King James, who adds that the plan was defeated by the indiscreet zeal of some of his own *fidèles*, who feared that Marlborough, were he once master of the situation, would put Anne on the throne instead of her father.

Whether, however, this supposed proposal was, or was not, the reason of Marlborough s dismissal, it is clear enough that he had resumed a secret correspondence with the banished king at St.-Germain, whom, not very long before, he had deserted. But so had most of the statesmen who surrounded William, even the admiral in whose hands the English reputation at sea was soon to be placed. The sins of the others were winked at while Marlborough was thus made an example of: perhaps because he was the most dangerous; perhaps because he had involved the princess in his treachery, persuading her to send a letter and make affectionate overtures to her father. Is it possible that it was this very letter which Burnet says was intercepted, inclosed most likely in one from Marlborough more distinct in its offers? Here is Anne's simple performance, a thing not calculated to do either harm or good:

I have been very desirous of some safe opportunity to make you a sincere and humble offer of my duty and submission, and to beg you will be assured that I am both truly concerned for the misfortunes of your condition, and sensible as I ought to be of my own unhappiness: as to what you may think I have contributed to it, if wishes could recall what is past, I had long since redeemed my fault. I am sensible that it would have been a great relief to me if I could have found means to have acquainted you earlier with my repentant thoughts, but I hope they may find the advantage of coming late — of being less suspected of insincerity than perhaps they would have been at any time before. It will be a great addition to the ease I propose to my own mind by this plain confession, if I am so happy as to find that it brings any real satisfaction to yours, and that you are as indulgent and easy to receive my humble submissions as I am to make them in a free disinterested acknowledgment of my fault, for no other end but to deserve and receive your pardon.

These involved and halting sentences by themselves could afford but little satisfaction to the anxious banished court at

St.-Germain. To say so much, yet to say so little, though easy to a confused intelligence, not knowing very well what it meant, is a thing which would have taxed the powers of the most astute conspirators. But there could be little doubt that a penitent princess thus ready to implore her father's pardon, would be a powerful auxiliary, with the country just then in the stage of natural disappointment which is prone to follow a great crisis, and that Marlborough was doubly dangerous with such a card in his hands to play.

A little pause occurred after his dismissal. The court by this time had gone to Kensington, out of sight and hearing of the Cockpit, Whitehall having been burned in the previous year. The princess continued, no doubt in no very friendly mood, to take her way to the suburban palace in the evenings and make one at her sister's game of basset, showing by her abstraction, and the traces of tears about her eyes, her state of depression yet revolt. But about three weeks after that great event, something suggested to Lady Marlborough the idea of accompanying her princess to the royal presence. It was strictly within her right to do so, in attendance on her mistress, and perhaps it was considered in the family council at the Cockpit that the existing state of affairs could not go on, and that it was best to end it one way or another. One can imagine the stir in the ante-chambers, the suppressed excitement in the drawing-room, when the princess, less subdued than for some weeks past, her eyes no longer red, nor the corners of her mouth drooping, came suddenly in out of the night, with the well-known buoyant figure after her, proud head erect and eyes aflame, her mistress's train upon her arm, but the air of a triumphant queen on her countenance. There would be a pause of consternation — and for a moment it would seem as if Mary, thus defied, must burst forth in wrath upon the culprit. What glances must have passed between the court ladies behind their fans! What whispers in the

QUEEN MARY OF MODENA.

ENGRAVED BY CHARLES STA..., AFTER THE PAINTING BY SIR PETER LELY,
IN POSSESSION OF EARL SPENCER.

corners! The queen, in the midst, pale with anger, restraining herself with difficulty; the princess, perhaps beginning to quake; but Sarah, undaunted, knowing no reason why she should not be there—"since to attend the princess was only paying her duty where it was owing.'

But next morning brought, as they must have foreseen it would bring, a royal missive, meant to carry dismay and terror, in which Mary commanded her sister to dismiss her friend and make instant submission. ' I tell you plainly Lady Marlborough must not continue with you in the circumstances in which her lord is," the queen wrote; "never anybody was suffered to live at court in my Lord Marlborough's circumstances." There is nothing undignified in Mary's letter. She was in all respects more capable of expressing herself than her sister, and she had so far right on her side that Lady Marlborough's appearance at court was little less than a deliberate insult to her. " I have all the reason imaginable to look upon you bringing her here as the strangest thing that ever was done, nor could all my kindness for you have hindered me showing you that moment, but I considered your condition, and that made me master of myself so far as not to take notice of it there," the queen said. The princess's condition had often to be taken into consideration, and perhaps she was not unwilling that her superiority in this respect to her childless sister should be fully evident. She was then within a few weeks of her confinement — not a moment when an affectionate and very dependent woman could lightly be parted from her bosom friend.

Thus the situation was brought to a climax. It was not to be expected, however, that Anne could have submitted to a mandate which in reality would have taken from her all power to choose her own friends; and her affections were so firmly fixed upon her beloved companion that it is evident life without Sarah would have been a blank to her. She answered in a letter stu-

3

diously compiled in defense both of herself and her retainer. "I am satisfied she cannot have been guilty of any fault to you, and it would be extremely to her advantage if I could here repeat every word that ever she had said to me of you in her whole life," says the princess; and she ends entreating her sister to "recall your severe command," and declaring that there is no misery "that I cannot readily resolve to suffer rather than the thought of parting with her." But things had gone too far to be stopped by any such appeal. The letter was answered by the lord chamberlain in person with a message forbidding Lady Marlborough to continue at the Cockpit. This was arbitrary in the highest degree, for the house was Anne's private property, bought for and settled upon her by Charles III.; and it was unreasonable, for Whitehall was lying in ruins, and Queen Mary's sight at Kensington could not be offended by the spectacle of the couple who had so annoyed her. The princess's spirit was roused. She wrote to her sister that she herself would be "obliged to retire," since such were the terms of her continuance, and sent immediately to the Duke of Somerset to ask for a lease of Sion House. It is said that William so far interfered in the squabble — in which indeed he had been influential all along — as to ask the duke to refuse this trifling favor. But of all English noble houses the proud Somersets were the last to be dictated to; and Anne established herself triumphantly in her banishment on the banks of the Thames with her favorite at her side.

A child was born a little later, and the queen paid Anne an angry visit of ceremony a day or two after the event, saying nothing to her but on the vexed subject. "I have made the first step by coming to you," Mary said, approaching the bed where the poor princess lay, sad and suffering, for her baby had died soon after its birth, "and I now expect you should make the next by removing Lady Marlborough." The princess, "trembling, and as white as her sheet," stammered forth her plaintive protest that this was the only thing in which she had disobliged her sister, and that "it was unreasonable to ask it of her," whereupon Mary, without another word, left the room and the house. It was the last time they ever met, unlikely as such a thing seemed. Anne made various overtures of reconciliation, but as unconditional obedience was promised in none, Mary's heart was not softened.

The only justification that can be offered for the queen's behavior was that they had been long separated and had little but the formal tie of relationship to bind them to each other. Anne had been but a child when Mary left England. They were both married and surrounded by other affections when they met again. They had so much resemblance of nature that each seems to have been capable of but one passion. It was Mary's good fortune to love her husband with all her heart — but to all appearance no one else. She had not a friend among all the ladies who had shared her life for years — no intimate or companion who could give her any solace when he was absent. Natural affection was not strong in their family. They had no mother, nor bond of common relationship except the father whom they both superseded. All this explains to a certain extent her coldness to Anne, and it is very likely she thought she was doing the best thing possible for her sister in endeavoring to separate her from an evil influence, an inferior who was her mistress. But this does not excuse the paltry and cruel persecution to which the younger sister was henceforward exposed. Every honor that belonged to her rank was taken from her, from the sentry at her door to the text upon her cushion at church. She was allowed no guard ; when she went into the country the rural mayors were forbidden to present addresses to her and pay the usual honors which mayors delight to pay. The great court ladies were given to understand that whoever visited her would not be received by the queen. A more irritating and miserable persecution could not be, nor one more lowering to the character of the chief performer in it.

Anne was but recovering from the illness that followed her confinement, and with which her sister's angry visit was supposed to have something to do, when another blow fell upon the band of friends. Marlborough was suddenly arrested and sent to the Tower. There was reason enough perhaps for his previous disgrace in the secret relations with St.-Germain which he was known to have resumed; but the charge afterward made was a purely fictitious one, and he and the other great personages involved had little difficulty in proving this innocence. The correspondence which took place while Lady Marlborough was in town with her husband on this occasion reveals Anne very clearly in her affectionate simplicity.

I hear Lord Marlborough is sent to the Tower; and though I am certain they have nothing against him, and expected by your letter it would be so, yet I was struck when I was told it; for methinks it is a dismal thing to have one's friends sent to that place. I have a thousand melancholy thoughts, and cannot help fearing they hinder you from coming to me; though how they can do that without making you a prisoner, I cannot imagine. I am just told by pretty good hands that as soon as the wind turns westerly there will be a guard set upon the prince and me. If you hear there is any such thing designed and that 'tis easy to you, pray let me see you before the wind changes: for afterward one does not know whether they will let one have opportunities of speaking to one another. But let them do what they please, nothing shall ever vex me, so I can have the satisfaction of seeing dear Mrs. Freeman; and I swear I would live on bread and water between four walls with her without repining; for so long as you continue kind, nothing can ever be a real mortification to your faithful Mrs. Morley, who wishes she may never enjoy a moment's happiness in this world or the next if ever she proves false to you.

Whether the wind proving "westerly" was a phrase understood between the correspondents, or if it had anything to do

with the event of the impending battle on which the fate of
England was hang.ng, it is difficult to tell. If it was used in
the latter sense, the victorious battle of La Hogue, by which all
recent discomfitures were redeemed, soon restored the government to calm and the consciousness of triumph, and made
conspiracy comparatively insignificant. Before this great deliverance was known, Anne had written a submissive letter
to her sister, informing her that she had now recovered her
strength "well enough to go abroad," and asking leave to pay
her respects to the queen. To which Mary returned a stern
answer declaring that such civilities were unnecessary as long
as her sister declined to do the thing required of her. Anne
sent a copy of this letter to Lady Marlborough, announcing, as
she was now "at liberty to go where I please by the queen
refusing to see me," her intention of coming to London to see
her friend, but this intention does not seem to have been
carried out. "I am very sensibly touched with the misfortune
that my dear Mrs. Freeman has had in losing her son, knowing
very well what it is to lose a child," the princess writes, "but
she, knowing my heart so well and how great a share I have
in all her concerns, I will not say any more on this subject for
fear of renewing her passion too much." Throughout this
separation these little billets were continually coming and
going, and we cannot do better than transcribe for the reader
some of those innocent letters, so natural and full of the
writer's heart.

Though I have nothing to say to my dear Mrs. Freeman I cannot
help inquiring how she and her Lord does. If it be not convenient for
you to write when you receive this, either keep the bearer till it is, or
let me have a word from you by the next opportunity when it is easy
to you, for I would not be a constraint to you at any time, much less
now when you have so many things to do and think of. All I desire to
hear from you at such a time is that you and yours are well, which
next to having my Lord Marlborough out of his enemies' power, is the

best news that can come to her, who to the last moment of her life will be dear to Mrs. Freeman's. . . .

I give dear Mrs. Freeman a thousand thanks for her letter which gives me an account of her concerns; and that is what I desire more to know than other news. I shall reckon the days and hours and think it very long till the time is out, both for your sake and my Lord Marlborough's, and that he may be at liberty and your mind at ease. And, dear Mrs. Freeman, don't say when I can see you if I come to town, therefore I ask which day will be most convenient for you. I confess I long to see you, but am not so unreasonable to desire that satisfaction till it is easy to you. I wish with all my soul that you may not be a true prophetess, and that it may soon be in our power to enjoy one another's company more than it has been of late, which is all I covet in this world. . . .

I am sorry with all my heart Mrs. Freeman meets with so many delays, but it is a comfort they cannot keep my Lord Marlborough in the Tower longer than the end of the term, and I hope when the Parliament sits care will be taken that people may not be clapt up for nothing, or else there will be no living in quiet for anybody but insolent Dutch and sneaking mercenary Englishmen. Dear Mrs. Freeman, farewell — be assured your faithful Mrs. Morley can never change, and I hope you do not in the least doubt of her kindness, which, if it be possible, increases every day, and that can never have an end but with her life. Mrs. Morley hopes her dear Mrs. Freeman will let her have the satisfaction of hearing again from her to-morrow. . . .

Dear Mrs. Freeman may easily imagine I cannot have much to say since I saw her. However, I must write two words, for though I believe she does not doubt of my constancy, feeling how base and false all the world is, I am of that temper I think I can never say enough to assure you of it. Therefore give me leave to assure you they can never change me. And there is no misery I cannot readily resolve to suffer rather than the thoughts of parting from you. And I do swear I would sooner be torn in pieces than alter this my resolution. My dear Mrs. Freeman, I long to hear from you.

This pretty correspondence changed a little, but only to grow more impassioned, when the princess had gone to Bath and the friends were less near each other.

Anne was, however, pursued by the royal displeasure even in her invalid journey to Bath, and no less a person than

Lord Nottingham, the lord chamberlain, was employed to warn the mayor of that city that his civilities to the princess were ill-timed. Such a disclosure of the family quarrel evinced a determination and bitterness which perhaps frightened even Lady Marlborough, courageous as she was; and she seems to have offered and even pressed her resignation as a means of making peace. But nothing altered the devotion of her faithful princess.

I really long to know how my dear Mrs. Freeman got home, and now I have this opportunity of writing she must give me leave to tell her if she should ever be so cruel as to leave her faithful Mrs. Morley she will rob her of all the joy and quiet of her life; for if that day should come, I could never enjoy a happy minute, and I swear to you I would shut myself up and never see a creature. If you do but remember what the queen said to me the night before your lord was turned out of all; then she began to pick quarrels; and if they should take off twenty or thirty thousand pounds, have I not lived upon as little before? When I was first married we had but twenty (it is true indeed the king was so kind to pay my debts) and if it should come to that again what retrenchment is there in my family I would not willingly make and be glad of that pretence to do it? Never fancy, my dear Mrs. Freeman, if what you fear should happen, that you are the occasion; no, I am very well satisfied, and so is the prince, too, that it would have been so however, for Caliban is capable of doing nothing but injustice; therefore rest satisfied you are noways the cause, and let me beg once more for God's sake that you would not mention parting more, no, not so much as think of it, and if you should ever leave me, be assured it would break your faithful Mrs. Morley's heart.

A still stronger expression of the same sentiment, with a little gleam of self-assertion and sense of injured dignity, follows, after the princess had, as would seem, taken counsel with her George. That heavy prince fully acquiesced at least, if nothing more, in his wife's devotion.

In obedience to dear Mrs. Freeman I have told the prince all she desired me, and he is so far from being of another opinion, if there had been occasion, he would have strengthened me in my resolutions, and we both beg you would never mention so cruel a thing again. Can you think either of us so wretched that for the sake of twenty thousand pounds, and to be tormented from morning to night with flattering knaves and fools, we should forsake those we have such obligations to, and that we are so certain we are the occasion of all their misfortunes? Besides, will you believe we will truckle to Caliban, who from the first moment of his coming has used us at that rate as we are sensible he has done, and that all the world can witness that will not let their interest weigh more with them than their reason? But suppose I did submit, and that the king could change his nature so much as to use me with humanity, how would all reasonable people despise me? How would that Dutch monster laugh at me, and please himself with having got the better! and which is much more, how would my conscience reproach me for having sacrificed it — my honor, reputation, and all the substantial comforts of this life — for transitory interest, which even to those who make it their idol, can never afford any real satisfaction, much less to a virtuous mind? No, my dear Mrs. Freeman, never believe that your faithful Mrs. Morley will ever submit. She can wait with patience for a sunshine day, and if she does not live to see it, yet she hopes England will flourish again. Once more give me leave to beg you would be so kind never to speak of parting more, for, let what will happen, that is the only thing that can make me miserable.

Such are the letters which Lord Macaulay describes as expressing "the sentiments of a fury in the style of a fish-woman." It was not indeed pretty to call great William Caliban, but Anne was fond of nicknames, and the king's personal appearance was not his strong point. To us the above outburst of indignation seems both natural and allowable. She had been subject to an inveterate and petty persecution — her little magnanimities had been answered by exactions. We are all so ready to believe that when a woman is involved she must be the offender, that most readers will have set down the insults to which Anne was subject to the account of Mary. But it is curious to note that in these letters all the blame is thrown upon the harsh brother-in-law, the Dutch monster, the alien, who had made so many strangers into English noblemen, and who identified Marlborough, among all the other courtiers who had been as

GUILLAUME III

De Roi et d'État loin a l'ordre [...]
Il [...]

WILLIAM III.

FROM COPPERPLATE ENGRAVING BY CORNELIS VERMEULEN, AFTER THE PAINTING
BY ADRIAAN VANDER WERFF.

little steadfast to him, as the object of a pertinacious persecution.
The princess says nothing of her sister. It is Caliban who is
capable of nothing but injustice. It is he who will laugh if he
gets the better of her. Anne's style is perhaps not quite worthy
of the Augustan age, but it is at least very intelligible and full
of little individual turns which are more characteristic than the
smoother graces. That she loved her friend with her whole
heart, that she had a generous contempt for interested motives,
and, humble as she was, a just sense of her own dignity, are all
abundantly and very simply manifest in them. They will give
to the impartial reader the impression of a natural and artless
character, with much generous feeling and much tender affec-
tionateness : tenacious of her rank and its observances, yet willing to throw all these trifles down at the feet of her friend.
Poor young lady ! When we recollect how constantly the
princess's "condition" had to be thought of, how her long
patience and many pains ended constantly in the little waxen
image of a dead baby and nothing more, who can wonder that
the world seemed falling to pieces about her when she was
threatened with the loss of the one strong sustaining prop upon
which she had hung from her childhood—the friend who had
helped her through all the first experiences of life, the companion who had amused so many weary days and made the
time pass as no one else could do !

All these miserable disputes, however, were ended in a
moment when brought into the cold twilight of a death-cham-
ber, where even kings and queens are constrained to see things
at their true value. Of all the royal personages in the kingdom, Mary's would have seemed to any outside spectator the
soundest and safest life. William had never been healthy, and
was consumed by the responsibilities and troubles into which he
had plunged. Anne had these ever-succeeding maternities to
keep her at a low level; but Mary was young, vigorous, and

happy — happy at least in her devotion to her husband and his love for her.   It was she, however, who, to the awe and consternation of the world, was cut down in her prime after a few days' illness, in the midst of her greatness.   Such a catastrophe no one could behold without the profoundest impulse of pity. Whatever she had done a week before, there she lay now helpless, all her splendors gone from her, the promise of a long career ended, and her partner left heartbroken upon the solitary throne to which she had given him the first right.

The sight of so forlorn a man,—so powerful, yet as impotent when his happiness was concerned as the meanest,—left thus heartbroken without courage or strength, his sole companion gone, and nothing but strangers, alien minds, and doubtful counselors round, is enough to touch any heart.   Anne, like the rest of the world, was shocked and startled by the sudden calamity. She sent anxious messages asking to be admitted to her sister's bedside ; and, when all was over, partly no doubt from policy, but we may be at least permitted to believe partly from good feeling, presented herself at Kensington Palace to show at least that rancor was not in her heart.   Unfortunately, there was no reconciliation between the sisters : the breach continued to the end of the queen's life, Burnet informs us.   But when the forlorn and solitary king was roused in his misery to receive his sister-in-law's message, a sort of peace was patched up between them over that unthought-of grave.   There was no longer any public quarrel or manifestation of animosity — and with this melancholy event the first half of Anne's history may be brought to an end.

CHAPTER II

THE QUEEN AND THE DUCHESS

A YEAR after the accession of William and Mary, and before any of the bitternesses and conflicts above recorded had openly begun, the only child of Anne on whose life any hopes could be built was born. Her many babies had died at birth or immediately after, and their quick and constant succession, as has been said, was the distinguishing feature of her personal life. But after the Revolution, when everything was settling out of the confusion of the crisis, and when as yet no further family troubles had disclosed the family rancors and disagreements, in the country air of Hampton Court, where the new king and queen were living, a little prince was born. Though he was sickly at first, like all the rest, he survived the dangers of infancy, and, called William after the king, and bearing from the first day of his life the title of Duke of Gloucester, was received joyfully by the nation at large and everybody concerned as the authentic heir to the crown. This child kept, it would seem, a little hold on the affections of the childless Mary during the whole course of the quarrel with his mother, bitter as it was, and continued an object of interest and kindness to William as long as he lived. The interposition of the quaint and precocious boy, with his big head, his premature enlightenment as to what it was and was not prudent to say, his sparkle of childish ambition, and all his old-fashioned ways, made a curious and welcome diversion in the troubled scene where nothing was happy, not even the child.

He was the chief occupation of Anne's life when comparative peace followed the warlike interval above related, and a cold and forced civility replaced the active hostilities which for years had been raging between the court and the household of the princess.

Anne has never got much credit for her forbearance and self-effacement at the critical moments of her career. But it is certain that she might have given William a great deal of trouble had she asserted her rights as Mary's successor, as she might also have done at the time of the first settlement. No doubt he would on both occasions have carried the day, and with this certainty the historians have been satisfied, without considering that a woman who was not of a lofty character, and who was a Stuart, must have felt it doubly bitter to find herself the subject of a gloomy brother-in-law who slighted her, and who, her rasher partizans did not hesitate to say, ought to have been her subject so long as he remained in England after her sister's death, and not she his. The absence of any attempt on her part to disturb or molest, nay, her little advances, her letters of condolence, and of congratulation the first time that a victory gave occasion for it, showed no inconsiderable magnanimity on the part of the prosaic princess—all the more that she had not been in the habit, as is usual among women, of putting the scorns she had suffered to another woman's account, and holding Mary responsible, but had uniformly attributed to the "Dutch monster," the Caliban of her correspondence, all the slights that were put on her—all the more that William did very little to encourage any overtures of friendship. He received her after his wife's death, and they are said by one of her attendants to have wept together when the unwieldy princess, then unable to walk, was carried in her chair into the very presence-chamber. But if a common emotion drew them together at this moment, it did not last; and in the diminished

THE DUKE OF GLOUCESTER.

ENGRAVED BY R. G. TIETZE, FROM MEZZOTINT BY JOHN SMITH AFTER THE PAINTING
BY SIR GODFREY KNELLER.

ceremonial of the bereaved court, Anne had but scant respect and no welcome. But she made no further complaint, and did what she could to keep on terms of civility at least with her brother-in-law, writing to him little letters of politeness, notwithstanding the disapproval of Lady Marlborough, who was of no such gentle temper, and the absence of all response from William. He, with all his foreign wars and home troubles, solitary, sad, broken in health and in life, had little heart, we may suppose, for those commonplace advances from a woman he had never been able to tolerate. But though Anne's relations with the king were scarcely improved, her position in respect to the courtiers who had abandoned her in her sister's lifetime was different indeed. Lady Marlborough describes this with her usual force.

And now it being quickly known that the quarrel was made up, nothing was to be seen but crowds of people of all sorts flocking to Berkeley House to pay their respects to the prince and princess; a sudden alteration which I remember occasioned the half-witted Lord Carnarvon to say one night to the princess as he stood close by her in the circle, " I hope your highness will remember that I came to wait upon you when none of this company did," which caused a great deal of mirth.

Meanwhile, the little boy, the heir of England, interposes his quaint little figure with that touch of nature which always belongs to a child, in the midst of all the excitement and dullness, awakening a certain interest even in the solitary and bereaved life of William, and filling his mother's house with tender anxieties and pleasures. He was sickly and feeble from his childhood, but early learned the royal lesson of self-concealment, and was cuffed and hustled by the anxious cruelty of love into the use of his poor little legs years after his contemporaries had been in full enjoyment of their liberty. It is characteristic of the self-absorbed and belligerent chronicler of the princess's household, whose narrative of all the quarrels and struggles of royal personages is so vivid, that she has very little to say about either the living or dying of the only child who was of such importance both to her mistress and to the country. His little existence is pushed aside in Lady Marlborough's record, and but for a little squabble over the appointment of the duke's " family," which she gives with great detail, we should scarcely have known from her that Anne had tasted that happiness of maternity which is so largely weighted with pains and cares.   But the story of little Gloucester's life, as found in the more familiar record of his waiting-gentleman, Lewis Jenkins, is both attractive and entertaining.   The little fellow seems to have been full of lively spirit and observation, active and restless in spite of his feebleness, full of a child's interest in everything about him, and of precocious judgment and criticism.   Some of the stories that are told of him put these gifts in a startling light.   " Who has taught you to say such words ? " his mother asks him when the child has been betrayed into innocent repetition of the oaths he had heard from his attendants.   The boy pauses before he replies.   " If I say Dick Dewey," he whispers to a favorite lady, " he will be sent down-stairs.   Mama, I invented them myself," he adds aloud.   The little being moving among worlds not realized, learning to play his little part, taking his cue from the countenances round him, forming his little policy in the twinkling of an eye, could not have had a better representative.   His careless indifference to his chaplain's religious services, but happy learning of little prayers and verses with the old lady to whom he takes a fancy, his weariness of lessons, yet eager interest in the diagrams that drop from Lewis Jenkins's pocket-book, and in all the bits of history he can induce his Welsh usher to tell him, and all the rest of his innocent childlike perversities, awaken in us an amused yet pathetic interest.   A troublesome, lovable, perverse, delightful child, not always easy to manage, constantly asking the most awkward

questions, full of ambition and energy and spirit and foolishness, the dull prince's somewhat tedious house brightens into
hope and sweetness so long as he is there.

In every respect this was the brightest moment of Anne's
life.   There was no longer any possibility of treating the next
heir to the crown, the mother of the only prince in whom the
imagination of England could take pleasure, with slighting or
contumely.   She was permitted to have her share of the honors
and comforts of English royalty.   St. James's old red-brick palace was given over to her as became her position ; and, what
was more wonderful, Windsor Castle, one of the noblest of
royal dwellings, became the country-house of Anne and her boy.
King William preferred Hampton Court, with its Dutch gardens,
in which he could imagine himself at home: the great feudal castle, erecting its massive towers from the crest of the gentle hill
which has the value of a much greater eminence in the midst of
the broad plain that sweeps forth in every direction round, was
not, apparently, to his taste.   And few prettier or more innocent scenes have been associated with its long history than those
in which little Gloucester was the chief actor.   He had a little
regiment of boys of his own age whom it was his delight to
drill and lead through a hundred mock battles and rapid skir-
mishings, mischievous little urchins who called themselves the
Duke of Gloucester's men, and played their little pranks like their
elders, as favorites will.   When he went to Windsor, four Eton
boys were sent for to be his playmates, one of them being young
Churchill, the son of Lady Marlborough.   The little prince chose
St. George's Hall for the scene of his mimic battles, and there
the little army stormed and besieged one another to their hearts'
content.   When his mother's marriage-day was celebrated, he received his parents with salvos of his small artillery, and, stepping
forth in his little birthday-suit, paid them his compliment: " Papa,
I wish you and Mama unity, peace, and concord, not for a time,

but forever," said the serious little hero.   One can fancy Anne, smiling and triumphant in her joy of motherhood, with her beautiful chestnut curls and sweet complexion and placid roundness, leaning on good George's arm,— her peaceful companion, with whom she had never a quarrel,— and admiring her son's infant wisdom.   It was their happy time: no cares of state upon their heads, no quarrels on hand, Sarah of Marlborough, let us hope, smiling too, and at peace with everybody, her own boy taking part in the ceremonial.

The little smoke and whiff of gunpowder, the little gunners at their toy artillery, the great hall still slightly athrill with the mimic salute, add something still to the boundless hopefulness of the scene ; for why should not this little English William grow up as great a soldier and more fortunate than his grim godfather, and subdue France under the feet of England, and be the conqueror of the world? All this was possible in those pleasant days.

On another occasion there was a great chapter of Knights of the Garter to witness the installation of little Gloucester in knightly state as one of the order.   The little figure, seven years old, seated under the noble canopywork in St. George's beautiful chapel, scarcely visible over the desk upon which his prayer-book was spread out, gazing with blue eyes intent, in all the gravity of a child, upon the great English nobles in their stalls around him, listening to the voices of the choristers pealing high into space, makes another touching picture.   King William himself had buckled the garter round the child's knee and hung the jewel about his neck,— St. George slaying his dragon, that immemorial emblem of the victory over evil ; and no doubt in the vague grandeur of childish anticipation, the boy felt himself ready to emulate the feat of the patron saint.   He was a little patriot too, eager to lend the aid of his small squadron to his uncle when William went away to the wars, and bringing a

GARDEN FRONT, HAMPTON COURT.

DRAWN BY JOSEPH PENNELL. ENGRAVED BY J. F. JUNGLING.

smile even upon that worn and melancholy face as he manœu-
vered his little company and showed how they would fight in
Flanders when the moment came. When William was threatened with assassination and the country woke up to feel that
though she did not love him it would be much amiss to lose him,
little Gloucester, at eight, was one of the most loyal. Taking
counsel with his little regiment, he drew up a memorial, written
out, no doubt, by the best master of the pen among them, with
much shedding of ink, if not of more precious fluid. "We, your
Majesty's subjects, will stand by you while we have a drop of
blood," was the address to which the Duke of Gloucester's men
set all their tiny fists. The little duke himself, not content with
this, added to it another address of his own :

I, your Majesty's most dutiful subject, had rather lose my life in your
Majesty's cause than in any man's else ; and I hope it will not be long
ere you conquer France.   GLOUCESTER.

Heroic little prince ! — a Protestant William, yet a gallant
and gentle Stuart. With this heart of enthusiasm and generous
valor in him, what might he not have done had he ever lived
to be king ? These marred possibilities, which are so common
in life, are almost the saddest things in it, and that must be a
heart very strong in faith that is not struck dumb by the withdrawal from earth's extreme need of so much faculty that
seemed created for her help and succor. It certainly awoke a
smile, and might have drawn an iron tear down William's cheek,
to see this faithful little warrior ready to "lose his life" in his
defense. And the good pair behind, George and Anne, who
had evidently suffered no treacherous suggestion to get to the
ear of the boy,— no hint that William was a usurper, and little
Gloucester had more right than he to be uppermost,— how
radiant they stand in the light of their happiness and hope! The
spectator is reluctant to turn the page to the coming gloom.

4

"When the Duke of Gloucester was arrived at an age to be put into men's hands," William's relenting and change of mind was proved by the fact that Marlborough, who had been in disgrace all these years, and whom only the constant favor of Anne had kept out of entire obscurity, was recalled into the front of affairs in order to be made "governor" of the young prince. It is true that this gracious act was partially neutralized by the appointment of Bishop Burnet as little Gloucester's tutor, a choice which was supposed to be as disagreeable to Anne as the other was happy. No distinct reason appears for this sudden and extraordinary change. Marlborough's connection with the family of the princess made him indeed peculiarly suitable to have the charge of her son, but William had not hitherto shown any desire to honor her likings; and this was not reason enough for all the other marks of favor bestowed upon him, bringing him back at once from private life and political disgrace to a position as high as any in the kingdom. Burnet himself did by no means relish the honor thus thrust upon him. He was almost disposed, he tells us, "to retire from the court and town," much as that would have cost him, rather than take upon him such a charge. But the pleasure of believing that "the king would trust that care only to me," and also an unexpected "encouragement" received from the princess, decided him to make the experiment. The little pupil was about nine when he came into the bishop's hands, and he gives the following account of his charge:

I had been trusted with his education now for two years, and he had made amazing progress. I had read over the Psalms, Proverbs, and Gospels with him, and had explained things that fell in my way very copiously; and was often surprised with the questions that he put to me, and the reflections that he made. He came to understand things relating to religion beyond imagination. I went through geography so often with him that he knew all the maps very particularly. I explained to him the forms of government in every country, with the in-

terests and trades of that country, and what was both bad and good in
it. I acquainted him with all the great revolutions that had been in the
world, and gave him a copious account of the Greek and Roman histories
of Plutarch's lives; the last thing I explained to him was the Gothic
constitution and the beneficiary and feudal laws: I talked of these
things at different times more than three hours a day; this was both
easy and delighting to him. The king ordered five of his chief ministers
to come once a quarter and examine the progress he made; they seemed
amazed both at his knowledge and the good understanding that appeared
in him; he had a wonderful memory and a very good judgment.

Poor little Gloucester! The genial bishop breaking down
all this knowledge into pleasant talks so that it should be "both
easy and delighting," and his lessons in fortification, which were
more delightful still, and his own little private princelike observation of men's faces and minds, were all to come to naught. On
his eleventh birthday, amid the feastings and joy, a sudden illness
seized him, and, a few days after, the promising boy had ended
his bright little career. As a matter of course, blame was attached to the doctor who attended him, and who had bled him
in the beginning of a fever; but this was almost universally the
case in the then state of medical science. "He was the only
remaining child," the bishop says, "of seventeen the princess
had borne, some to the full time and the rest before it. She
attended on him during his sickness with great tenderness, but
with a grave composedness that amazed all who saw it. She
bore his death with a resignation and piety that were indeed
very singular." It would be small wonder indeed if Anne had
been altogether crushed by such a calamity. It is said by
some historians of the Jacobite party that her mind was overwhelmed by a sense of her guilt toward her own father, and of
just judgment executed upon her in the loss of her child, and
that she immediately wrote to James, pouring out her whole
heart in penitence, and pledging herself to support the claims
of her brother should she ever come to the throne. This letter,

however, was never found, and does not seem to be vouched for by witnesses beyond suspicion. But for the fact that Anne was stricken to the dust, no parent will need any further evidence. Her good days and hopes were over; henceforward, when she wrote to her dearest friend in the old confidential strain, it was as "your poor unfortunate Morley" that the bereaved mother signed herself. Nothing altered these sad adjectives. She felt herself as poor and unfortunate in her unutterable loss when she was queen as if she had been the humblest woman that ever lost an only child.

Marlborough was absent when his little pupil fell ill, but hurried back to Windsor in time to see him die. It was etiquette in those days that in case of a death the survivors should instantly leave the place in which it had happened, leaving the dead in possession, to lie in state there and receive the homage of curious or interested spectators. But Anne would not be persuaded to leave the place where her child was, and, four or five days after, the little prince was carried solemnly by torchlight through the summer woods, through Windsor Park, and by the river, and under the trees of Richmond, to Westminster: a silent procession pouring slowly through the odorous August night. His little body lay in state in Westminster Hall—a noble chamber for such a tiny sleeper—for five days more, when it was laid with the kings in the great abbey which holds all the greatest of England. A more heartrending episode is not in history.

William did not take any notice of the announcement of the death for a considerable time, which embarrassed the ambassador at Paris greatly on the subject of mourning, and has given occasion for much denunciation of his hardness and heartlessness. When he answered at last, however—though this was not till more than two months after, in a letter to Marlborough —it was with much subdued feeling. "I do not think it neces-

THE DUKE OF GLOUCESTER

sary to employ many words,' he writes, "in expressing my surprise and grief at the death of the Duke of Gloucester. It is
so great a loss to me as well as to all England, that it pierces
my heart with affliction." It seems impossible that the loss of a
child who had shown so touching an allegiance to himself should
not have moved him; but perhaps there was in him, too, a
touch of satisfaction that the rival pair who had been thorns in
his flesh since ever he came to England, were not to have the
satisfaction of founding a new line. At St.-Germain the satisfaction was more marked still, and it was supposed that the most
dangerous obstacle in the way of the young James Stuart was removed by the death of his sister's heir. We know now how futile
that anticipation was; but at the time this was not so clear, and
the anxiety of the English parliament to secure before William's
death a formal abjuration of the so-called Prince of Wales shows
that the hope was not without foundation.

This and the new and exciting combination of European affairs produced by what is called the " Spanish Succession," occupied all minds during the two years that remained of William's
suffering life. It was a moment of great excitement and uncertainty. Louis XIV., into whose hands, as seemed likely, a sort
of universal power must fall if his grandson were permitted to
succeed to the throne of Spain, had just vowed at the death-bed
of James his determination to support the claims of the exile's
son, and, on James's death, had proclaimed the boy King of England. Thus England had every reason of personal irritation and
even alarm for joining in the alliance against the threatening
supremacy of France, whose power—had she been allowed
to place one of her princes peaceably on the Spanish throne, to
which the rich Netherlands still belonged—would have been
paramount in Europe. It was on the eve of the great struggle
that William died. With a determination equal to that with
which he had made head against failing fortune in many a bat-

tle-field, he fought for his life, which, at such a crisis, was doubly
important to the countries of his birth and of his crown, and to
the cause of the Protestant religion and all that we have been
taught to consider as freedom throughout Europe. There is
something pathetic in the struggle, in the statement of his case,
under one name or another as a private individual, that there
might be no doubt as to the frankness of the opinions which he
caused to be made among the great physicians of Europe.
His life in itself could not have been a very happy or desirable
one. He had no longer his popular and beloved Mary to leave
behind him in England as his representative when he set out
for the wars, and there were few in England whom he trusted
fully, or who trusted him. To die at the beginning of a
great European struggle, leaving the dull people whom he
disliked to take his place in England, and the soldier whom
he had crushed and subdued and sternly held in the shade as
long as he was able, to assume his baton, and win the victories
it had never been William's fortune to gain, must have been
bitter indeed. It would appear even that he had entertained
some idea of disturbing the natural order of events to prevent
this, and that it had been suggested to the Electress Sophia,
after poor little Gloucester's death, that her family should
at once be nominated as his immediate successors, to the
exclusion of Anne, a proposal which the prudent electress
evaded with great skill and ingenuity by representing that
the Prince of Wales — who must surely have learned, he and
his counselors, wisdom from the failure of his father — was the
natural heir, and would, no doubt, do well enough on a trial.
Bishop Burnet denies that such a design was ever entertained,
but Lord Dartmouth, in his notes upon Burnet, gives the following very distinct evidence on the subject :

I do not know how far the Whig party would trust a secret of that
consequence to such a blab as the bishop was known to be : but the

Dukes of Bolton and Newcastle both proposed it to me, and used the strongest arguments to induce me to come into it; which was that it would be making Lord Marlborough King at least for the time if the Princess succeeded; and that I had reason to expect nothing but ill-usage during such a reign. Lord Marlborough asked me afterward in the House of Lords if I had ever heard of such a design. I told him Yes, but did not think it very likely. He said it was very true: but by God if ever they attempted it we would walk over their bellies.

Thus until the last moment Anne's position would seem to have been menaced; but a more impossible scheme was never suggested, for even the idea of Marlborough's triumph was unable to raise the smallest party against the princess, and to the country in general she was the object of a kind of enthusiasm. The people loved everything in her, even the fact that she was not clever, which of itself is often highly ingratiating with the masses. William, it is said, with a magnanimity which was infinitely to his credit, named Marlborough as his most fit successor in the command of the allied armies before he died. The formal abjuration of the Prince of Wales was made by Parliament only just in time to have his assent, and then all obstacles were removed out of the princess's way. It was thought by the populace that everything brightened for the new reign. There had been an unexampled continuance of gloomy weather, bad harvests, and clouds and storms. But to great Queen Anne the sun burst forth, the gloom dispelled, the country broke out into gaiety and rejoicing. A new reign full of new possibilities has always something exhilarating in it. William's greatness was marred by externals and never heartily acknowledged by the mass of the people, but Anne had many claims upon the popular favor. She was a woman, and a kind and simple one. That desertion of her father which some historical writers have condemned so bitterly, had no great effect upon the contemporary imagination, nor, so far as can be judged, upon her own; and it was the only offense that could be alleged

against her.   She had been unkindly treated and threatened
with wrong, which naturally made the multitude strenuous in her
cause; and everything conspired to make her accession happy.
She was only thirty-seven, and though somewhat unwieldy in
person, still preserved her English comeliness, her abundant,
beautiful hair, and, above all, the melodious voice by which even
statesmen and politicians were impressed.   " She pronounced
this," says Bishop Burnet, describing her address to the Privy
Council when they first presented themselves before her, " as
she did all her other speeches, with great weight and authority,
and with a softness of voice and sweetness in the pronunciation
that added much life to all she spoke."   The commentators
who criticize so sorely the bishop's chronicles are in entire
agreement with him on this subject.   " It was a real pleasure
to hear her," says Lord Dartmouth, " though she had a bashful-
ness that made it very uneasy to herself to say much in public."
Speaker Onslow unites in the same testimony: " I have heard
the queen speak from the throne, and she had all the author
says here.   I never saw an audience more affected ; it was a
sort of charm.   She received all that came to her in so gracious
a manner that they went from her highly satisfied with her
goodness and her obliging deportment; for she hearkened
with attention to everything that was said to her."   Thus all
smiled upon Anne in the morning of her reign.   Her coronation was marked with unusual splendor and enthusiasm, and
though the queen herself had to be carried in a chair to the
Abbey, her state of health being such that she could not walk,
this did not affect the splendid ceremonial in which even to the
Jacobites themselves there was little to complain of, since their
hopes that Anne's influence might advance her father's young
son to the succession after her were still high, notwithstanding
that the settlement of the crown upon Sophia of Brunswick
and her heirs had already been made.

ANNA D. G. ANGLIÆ, SCOTIÆ,
FRANCIÆ ⊕ HIBERNIÆ REGINA.

QUEEN ANNE.

FROM COPPERPLATE ENGRAVING BY PIETER VAN GUNST, AFTER THE PAINTING
BY SIR GODFREY KNELLER.

It is needless for us to attempt a history of the great war which was one of the most important features in Anne's reign. No student of history can be ignorant of its general course, nor of the completeness with which Marlborough's victories crushed the exorbitant power of France and raised the prestige of England. There is no lack of histories of the great general and his career of victory: how he out-fought, out-marched, and out-generaled all his rivals, and scarcely in his ten years of active warfare encountered one check; how, though he did not accomplish the direct object for which all the bloodshed and toil were undertaken, he yet secured such respect for the English name and valor as renewed our old reputation and made all interference with our natural settlement or intrusion into our private economy impossible forever. "What good came of it at last?" says the poet. But the inquiry, though so plausible, appealing at once to humanity and common sense, is not perhaps so hard to answer as it seems. Up to this time it has been impossible to procure in the intercourse of nations any other effectual arbiter but the sword: a terrible one, indeed, but apparently as yet the only means of keeping a check upon the rapacity of some, and protecting the weakness of others. At all events, whatever individual opinion may be on the point now, there was a unanimous conviction then, and no one doubted at the opening of the war that it was most necessary and just. And of its conduct there has been but one opinion. Contemporaries accused Marlborough of every conceivable wickedness,—of peculation, treachery, even personal cowardice; but no one ventured to say that he was not a great general. And as we have got further and further from the infuriated politics of his time, his gifts and graces, his wisdom and moderation, as well as his wonderful military genius, have been done more and more justice to. Coxe, his special biographer, may be supposed to look with partiality upon his hero; but this cannot be said of more recent writers,—of Lord Stanhope in his tolerant and sensible history, or of Dr. Hill Burton in his sagacious volumes on the reign of Queen Anne.

It is, however, with Marlborough's wife and not with himself that we are chiefly concerned, and with the stormy course of Anne's future intercourse with her friend rather than the battles that were fought in her name. It is said that by the time she came to the throne her faithful affection to her lifelong companion had begun to be impaired, but the date of the first beginning of their severance will probably never be determined, nor its immediate cause. Miss Strickland professes to have ascertained that certain impatient words used by Sarah of Marlborough, which were overheard by the queen, were the occasion of the breach; but as there is no very satisfactory foundation for the story, and it is added that Anne kept her feelings undisclosed for long after, we may dismiss the legend as possible enough, but no more.

All the great hopes which the pair must have formed seemed likely to be fulfilled in the early part of Queen Anne's reign. A very short time after her accession, Marlborough, who had at once entered upon the conduct of foreign affairs and the preparations for war, according to William's appointment, received the garter which Anne and her husband had vainly asked for him in the previous reign; and when he returned from his first campaign, a dukedom was bestowed upon him, with many pretty expressions on Anne's part.

Indeed, the queen's gift of "writing pretty, affectionate letters," which was the only thing, according to the duchess's opinion of her expressed in later days, that she could do well, is still abundantly proved by the correspondence. Anne was as anxious as ever to serve and please her friend and favorite. She prays God, in her little note of congratulation after the siege of Bonn in 1703, to send Marlborough "safe home to his and my

dear adored Mrs. Freeman," with all the grace of perfect sympathy; for the great duke was as abject in his adoration of that
imperious, bewitching, and triumphant Sarah as the queen herself. With the tenderest recollection of her friend's whims, the
queen gave her the rangership of Windsor Park (strange office for a woman to hold!) in which was included "a lodge in
the great park," which the duchess describes as "a very agreeable place to live in," . . . 'remembering that when we used in
former days to ride by it, I had often wished for such a place,"
although it was necessary to turn out Portland, King William's friend and favorite, in order to replace him by Lady
Marlborough; no doubt, however, this summary displacement
of the Dutchman added to the pleasure both of giving and
receiving. Lady Marlborough had a multiplicity of other
offices in addition to this,—such as those of mistress of the
robes, groom of the stole, and keeper of the privy purse,—
offices, however, which she had virtually held for years in the
household of the princess. All these brought in a great deal
of money, a matter to which she was never indifferent; and
along with the dukedom, the queen bestowed upon Marlborough a pension of £5000 a year; so that the resources of
the new ducal house were abundant. They would seem by
their posts and perquisites alone to have had an income between
them not far short of £50,000 a year, an enormous sum for
those times, not to speak of less legitimate profits — presents
from contractors, and percentages on the pay of the troops,
which Marlborough took, as everybody did, as a matter of
course, though it was afterward charged against him as if he
had invented the custom. The queen also promised a little
fortune to each of their daughters as they married — a promise
certainly fulfilled in the case of Henrietta, who married the son
of Godolphin, thus uniting the colleagues in the closest family
bonds. Anne also offered a pension of £2000 a year to the

duchess from the privy purse, a bounty declined at first, but of which afterward, in the final breaking up of their relations, Sarah was mean enough to demand the arrears, amounting to no less a sum than £18,000. Thus every kind of gift and favor was pressed upon the royal favorite in the early days of Anne's reign.

Before this the means of the pair had been but small. Marlborough had been long deprived of all preferment, and the duchess informs us that she had discharged in the princess's household all the offices for which afterward she was so highly paid on an allowance of £400 a year. It was for this reason that the dukedom was unwelcome to her. " I do agree with you," her husband writes to her, "that we ought not to wish for a greater title till we have a better estate," and he assures her that "I shall have a mind to nothing but as it may be easy to you." It was in this strain that the great conqueror always addressed his wife, and it would be difficult to say which of her two adorers, her husband or her queen, showed the deepest devotion. When Marlborough set out for his first campaign in the war which was to cover him with glory, and in which for the first time he had full scope, this is how he writes to the companion of his life (she had gone with him to Margate to see him embark):

It is impossible to express with what a heavy heart I parted from you when I was by the water's side. I could have given my life to have come back though I knew my own weakness so much that I durst not, for I know I should have exposed myself to the company. I did for a great while with a perspective glass look out upon the cliffs in hopes I might have had one sight of you. We are now out of sight of Margate and I have neither soul nor spirits, but I do at this time suffer so much that nothing but being with you can recompense it.

These lover-like words were written by a man of fifty-two to his wife of forty-two, to whom he had been married for nearly a quarter of a century. In all the pauses of these wars, amid the

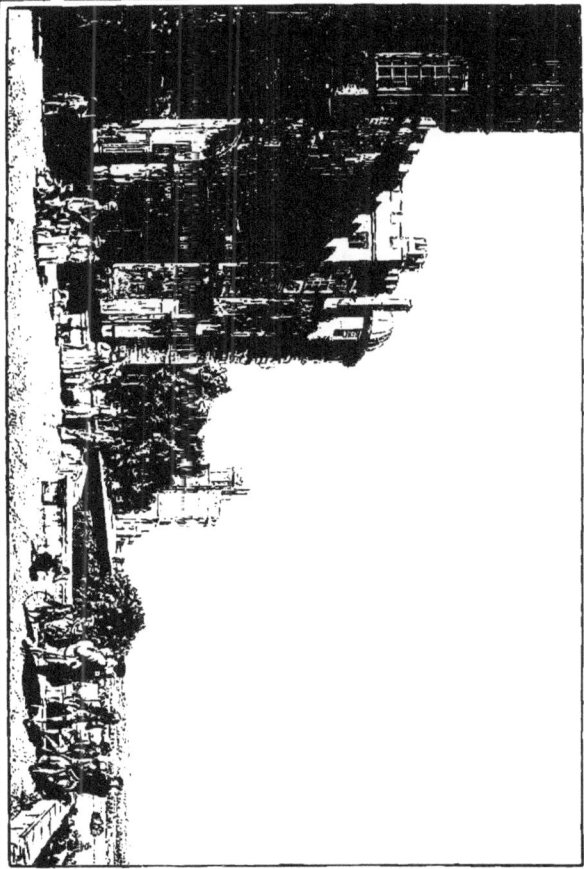

WINDSOR TERRACE, LOOKING WESTWARD.

ENGRAVED BY J. W. EVANS AFTER AQUATINT BY P. SANDBY

plans and combinations of armies, and all the hard thinking and
hard fighting, the perpetual activity and movement of his life
for the next ten years, the same voice of passionate attachment,
love, and longing penetrates for us the tumults of the time.
She was flattered to the top of her bent both by husband and
mistress ; and it is not much to be wondered at if she came to
think herself indispensable and above all law.

In the midst, however, of this prosperity and quickly growing greatness, the same crushing calamity which had previously
fallen upon Anne, overwhelmed these companions of her life.
Their only son, a promising boy of seventeen, died at Cambridge, and both father and mother were bowed to the dust.
The queen's letter on this occasion expresses her sense of
yet another melancholy bond between them. It is evident
that she had offered to go to her friend in her affliction. " It
would be a great satisfaction to your poor unfortunate faithful
Morley if you would have given me leave to come to St.
Alban's," she writes, " for the unfortunate ought to come to
the unfortunate." With a heavy heart Marlborough changed
his will, leaving the succession of the titles and honors, so suddenly deprived of all value to him, to the family of his eldest
daughter, and betook himself sadly to his fighting, deriving
a gleam of satisfaction from the thought that other children
might yet be granted to him, yet adjuring his wife to bear their
joint calamity with patience, whatever might befall. She herself
says nothing on this melancholy subject. Perhaps in her old age,
as she sat surveying her life, that great but innocent sorrow no
longer seemed to her of the first importance in a record crossed
by so many tempests—or perhaps it was of so much importance
that she would not trust herself to speak of it at all. The partizans of the exiled Stuarts were eager to point out how both
she and her mistress had suffered the penalty of their sin
against King James and his son, by being thus deprived of

their respective heirs.   It was a "judgment"—a thing dear
to the popular imagination and most easily concluded upon
at all times.

It would not seem, however, that this natural drawing of
"the unfortunate to the unfortunate" had the effect it might
have had in further cementing the union of the queen and
the duchess.   The

little rift within the lute
That by and by will make the music mute

began to be apparent shortly after, though not at first showing
itself by any lessening of warmth or tenderness.   The existence
of a division of opinion is the first thing visible.   " I cannot help
being extremely concerned that you are so partial to the Whigs,
because I would not have you and your poor unfortunate faithful Morley differ in the least thing.   And, upon my word, my
dear Mrs. Freeman," adds Queen Anne, "you are mightily mistaken in your notion of a true Whig.   For the character you
give of them does not in the least belong to them."

We need not discuss here the difference between the meaning of the names Tory and Whig as understood then and now.
Lord Mahon and Lord Macaulay both consider a complete
transposition of terms to be the easiest way of making the
matter clear, but in one particular at least this seems scarcely
necessary ; for the Tories, then as now, were emphatically the
church party, which was to Anne the only party in which
safety could be found.   The queen had little understanding of
history or politics in the wider sense of the words, but she was
an excellent churchwoman, and in the sentiments of the Tory
leaders she found, when brought into close contact with them,
something more in accord with her own, the one sympathy in
which her bosom friend had been lacking.

"'These were men who had all a wonderful zeal for the Church,
a sort of public merit that eclipsed all others in the eye of the

Queen. . . . For my own part," the duchess adds, " I had not
the same prepossessions. The word *Church* had never any
charm for me in the mouths of those who made the most noise
with it, for I could not perceive that they gave any other proof
of their regard for the thing than a frequent use of the word, like
a spell to enchant weak minds, and a persecuting zeal against
dissenters and against the real friends of the Church who would
not admit that persecution was agreeable to its doctrine."

This difference had not told for very much so long as neither
the queen nor her friend had any share in public affairs, but it
became strongly operative now. How much the queen had actually to do with the business of the nation, and how entirely
it depended upon the influence brought to bear upon her limited mind who should be the guide of England at this critical
moment, is abundantly evident from every detail of history.
Queen Victoria, great as her experience is, and notwithstanding
the respectful attention which all classes of politicians naturally
give to her opinion, changes her ministry only when the majority
in Parliament requires it, and has only the very limited choice
which the known and acknowledged heads of the two parties
permit when she transfers office and power from one side to the
other. But Queen Anne had no compact body of statesmen,
one replacing the other as occasion required, to deal with; but
put in here one high official and there another, according as
intrigue or impulse gained the upper hand.

There is something about a quarrel of women which excites
the scorn of every chronicler, an insidious contempt for the
weaker half of the creation which probably no one would own
to, lying dormant in the minds of the race generally, even of
women themselves. Had Anne been a king of moderate abili-
ties, and Marlborough the friend and guide to whom he owed
his prosperity and fame, the relationship would have been noble
and honorable to both; and when the struggle began, the

strenuous offorts of the great general to secure the coöperation of ministers with whom he could work, and whose support
would have helped toward the carrying out of his great plans
for the glory of his country and the destruction of her enemies,
would, whether the historical critic approved of them or not,
have at least secured his respect and a dignified treatment.
But when it is Sarah of Marlborough, with all the defects of
temper that we know in her, who, while her lord fights abroad,
has to fight for him at home, to scheme his enemies out of, and
his friends into, power, to keep her hold upon her mistress by
every means that her imagination can devise, the idea that some
nobler motive than mere self-aggrandizement may be in the
effort occurs to no one, and the hatred of political enmity is
mingled with all the ridicule that spiteful wit can discharge
upon a feminine squabble.   Lady Marlborough was far from
being a perfect woman.   She had a fiery temper and a stinging
tongue.   When she was thwarted at the very moment of apparent victory, and found herself impotent where she had been
all-powerful, her fury was like a torrent against which there was
no standing.   But with these patent defects it ought to be allowed her that the object for which she struggled was not only
a perfectly legitimate, but a noble one.   What the great William
had spent his life and innumerable campaigns in endeavoring to
do, against all the discouragements of frequent failure, Marlborough was doing, with a matchless and almost unbroken success.   It was no shame to either the general or the general's
wife to believe, as William did, that this was the greatest work
of the time, and could alone secure the safety of England as
well as of her allies.   And the gallant stand of Lady Marlborough for the party and the statesmen who were likely to
carry out this object, deserved some better interpretation from
history than it has ever received.

And it cannot be said that there was anything petty in Anne's

THE DUKE OF MARLBOROUGH.

ENGRAVED BY J. H. E. WHITNEY, FROM AN ENGRAVING BY PIETER VAN GUNST,
AFTER PAINTING BY ADRIAAN VANDER WERFF.

public acts while she remained under the influence of her first friend. The beginning of her reign showed no ignoble spirit. One of the first things the queen did was to abolish the old and obstinate practice of selling places, which had hitherto been accepted as the course of nature; so much so that when Marlborough fell into disgrace under King William, he had been bidden to "sell or dispose of" the places he held, and the princess had herself informed Sarah at least on one occasion of vacancies, in order that her friend should have the profit of filling them up. "Afterwards, I began to consider in my own mind this practice," the lady says; but whether she took the initiative in so honorable a measure, it would be rash to pronounce upon the authority of her own word alone. It certainly, however, was one of the first acts of the queen, and the credit of such a departure from the use and wont of courts should at least be allowed to the new reign. Anne did various other things for which there was no precedent. As soon as her civil list was settled, she gave up voluntarily £100,000 a year to aid the public expenses, then greatly increased by the war, and, shortly after, she made a still more important and permanent sacrifice by giving up the ecclesiastical tribute of first-fruits and tithes; namely, the first year's stipend of each cure to which a new incumbent was appointed, and the tenth of all livings — to which the crown, as succeeding the Pope in the headship of the church, had become entitled. Her object was the augmentation of small livings and better provision for the necessities of the church, and there can be little doubt that this act at least was exclusively her own. The fund thus formed continues to this day under the name of Queen Anne's Bounty, but unfortunately remained quite inefficacious during her reign, in consequence of various practical difficulties; and it has never been by any means the important agency she intended it to be. But the intention was munificent and the desire sincere.

Throughout her life the church was the word which most moved Anne. She was willing to do anything to strengthen it, and to sacrifice any one, even as turned out her dear friend, in its cause.

The first subject which quickened a vague and suspicious disagreement into opposition was the bill against what was called occasional conformity, a bill which was aimed at the dissenters and abolished the expedient formerly taken advantage of in order to admit nonconformists to some share in public life — of periodical compliance with the ceremonies of the church. The new law not only did away with this important "easement," but was weighted with penal enactments against those who, holding office under government, should be present at any conventicle or assembly for worship in any form but that of the Church of England. Upon this subject the queen writes as follows:

I must own to you that I never cared to mention anything on this subject to you because I knew you would not be of my mind, but since you have given me the occasion, I can't forbear saying that I see nothing like persecution in the bill. You may think it is a notion Lord Nottingham has just put into my head, but upon my word it is my own thought. I promise my dear Mrs. Freeman faithfully I will read the book she sent me, and beg she will never let differences of opinion hinder us from living together as we used to do. Nothing shall ever alter your poor unfortunate faithful Morley, who will live and die with all truth and tenderness yours.

As the differences go on increasing, however, Queen Anne gradually changes her ground. At first she "hopes her not agreeing with anything you say will not be imputed to want of value, esteem, or tender kindness, for my dear, dear Mrs. Freeman"; but at last, as the argument goes on, plucks up a spirit and finds courage enough to declare roundly that whenever public affairs are in the hands of the Whigs, "I shall think the Church beginning to be in danger." Thus the political situation became more and more difficult, and gradually embittered even the personal relations between the friends, and the duchess had not even the support of her husband in her political preferences. He had himself belonged to the moderate Tory party, and, even though they thwarted and discouraged him, showed no desire to throw himself into the arms of the Whigs, whither his wife would so fain have led him. He was almost as little encouraging to her in this point as the queen was. "I know," he says, "they would be as unreasonable as the others in their expectations if I should seek their friendship,—for all parties are alike." It was thus a hard part she had to play between the queen's determination that the Whigs were the enemies of the church,¹ and her husband's conviction that all parties were alike. He, perhaps, was the more hard to manage of the two. He voted for the occasional conformity bill, against which she was so hot, and trusted in Harley, who indeed owed his first beginning to Marlborough's favor, but whom the duchess saw through. In young St. John, too, the great general had perfect faith; "I am very confident he will never deceive you," he wrote to Godolphin. Thus the husband warmed in his bosom the vipers that were to sting him and bring a hasty end to his career. He, too, remained obstinately indifferent, while she stormed and entreated and wrote a hundred letters and used every art both of war and peace in vain. It is easy to see how this perpetual letter-writing, her determination to prove that her correspondent was in error and she right, and her continual reiteration of the same charges and reproaches, must have exasperated the queen and troubled Marlborough, in the midst of the practical difficulties of his career. But yet there are many points on which Sarah has a just claim to our sympathy. For she foresaw what actually did happen, and perceived whither the current was tending, but was refused any credit for her prognostications or help in subduing the dangerous forces she dreaded. How irritating this position must have been to a fiery temper it is needless to point out, and the duchess would not permit herself to be silenced by either husband or queen. Lord Macaulay's description of the astonishing state of affairs which compelled two of the ablest statesmen in Europe to have recourse for the conduct of the imperial business to the influence of one woman over another, was thus far less true even than it seems on the surface; for Sarah of Marlborough suspected the real state of the case when no one else did, fighting violently against her husband's enemies before they had disclosed themselves, and her final overthrow was as much the result of a new tide in political affairs as of the straining of the personal relations between her and her queen.

Meanwhile, Marlborough was going on in his career of conquest. It was a very costly luxury; but the pride of England had never been so fed with triumphs. Queen Anne was in her closet one day at Windsor, a little turret-chamber with windows on every side looking over the green and fertile valley of the Thames, with all the trees in full summer foliage and the harvest beginning to be gathered in from the fields, when there was brought to her a scrap of crumpled paper bearing upon it the few hurried lines which told of the "glorious victory" of the battle of Blenheim. It had been torn off in haste from a memorandum book on the field, and was scribbled over with an inn-reckoning on the other side. The commotion it caused was not one of unmixed joy; for though the queen wrote her thanks and congratulations, and there was a great thanksgiving service at St. Paul's, which she attended in state, the party in power did all that in them lay to depreciate the importance of the victory. When, however, Marlborough appeared in England with his prisoners and trophies,—a marshal of France among the former,—and many standards taken in the field, the popular sentiment burst all bounds, and his reception was enthusiastic. The crown lands of Woodstock were bestowed upon him as a further reward, and the queen herself commanded that a palace should be built upon the estate at the expense of the crown, to be called Blenheim in commemoration of the extraordinary victory.   A curious relic of ancient custom religiously carried out to the present day .was involved in this noble gift.   The quit-rent which every holder of a royal fief has to pay, was appointed to be a banner embroidered with three *fleurs-de-lis*, the arms then borne by France, to be presented on every anniversary of the battle.   Not very long ago the present writer accompanied a French lady of distinction through some part of Windsor Castle under the guidance of an important member of the queen's household.   When the party came into the armory, on each side of which, a vivid spot of color, hung a little standard fresh in embroidery of gold, the kind cicerone smiled, and whispered aside, "We need not point out these to her."   One of them was the Blenheim, the other the Waterloo banner, both yearly acknowledgments, after the old feudal fashion, for fiefs held of the crown.

Among the honors done to Marlborough at this triumphant moment, when, an English duke, a prince of the Holy Roman Empire, and, still more splendid title, the greatest soldier of his time, he came home in glory to England, were the verses with which Addison saluted him.   There were plenty of odes piping to all the winds in his honor, but this alone worthy of record. Every reader will recollect the simile of the great angel who "drives the furious blast;"

> And, pleased the Almighty's orders to perform,
> Rides in the whirlwind, and directs the storm.

The compliment might be supposed to be somewhat magnificent even for the greatest of commanders.   And yet whatever

5*

Marlborough's faults may have been, his attitude during this
wonderful war is scarcely too splendidly described by the image
of a calm and superior spirit beholding contemporary events
from a higher altitude than that of common humanity, executing
vengeance and causing destruction without either rage or fear,
in serene fulfilment of a great command and in pursuance of
a mighty purpose. His unbroken temper, his patience and
courtesy in the midst of all contentions, the firm composure with
which he supports all the burdens thrown upon him, appeals
from home as well as necessities abroad, might well suggest a
spirit apart, independent, not moved like lesser men. No man
ever bore so many conflicting claims more calmly. Even the
adjurations, the commands, the special pleadings of his "dearest
soul" do not lead him a step farther than he thinks wise.
"When I differ from you," he says, "it is not that I think those
are in the right whom you say are always in the wrong, but it
is that I would be glad not to enter into the unreasonable rea-
soning of either party; for I have trouble enough for my little
head in the business which of necessity I must do here." There
could not be a greater contrast than between the commotion
and whirlwind that surrounds Duchess Sarah and the great
general's calm.

It is not necessary for our purpose to enter into those
changes of ministry which first temporarily consolidated the
Marlborough interest and afterward wrought its destruction,
nor into the intrigues by which Harley and St. John gradually
secured the reins of state. It is not to be supposed that these
fluctuations were wholly owing to the influences brought to
bear upon the queen; but that her prevailing disposition to
uphold the party which to her represented the church kept the
continuance of the war and the foreign policy of the country in
constant danger, there can be no doubt. It is only in 1707,
however, that we are made aware of the entry of a new actor

upon the scene, in the person of a smooth and noiseless woman, always civil, always soft-spoken, apologetic, and plausible,
whose sudden appearance in the vivid narrative of her great
rival is in the highest degree dramatic and effective. This was
the famous Abigail who has given her name, somewhat injuri-
ously to her own position, to the class of waiting-women ever
since. She was in reality bedchamber-woman to the queen—
a post now very far removed from that of a waiting-maid, and
even then by no means on a level, notwithstanding the duchess's
scornful phrases, with that of the class which ever since has
been distinguished by Mrs. Hill's remarkable name. Her introduction altogether, and the vigorous *mise en scène* of this
new episode in history, are fine examples of the graphic power
of Duchess Sarah. Her suspicions, she informs us, were roused
by the information that Abigail Hill, a relation of her own, and
placed by herself in the royal household, had been married
without her knowledge to Mr. Masham, who was one of the
queen's pages ; but there are allusions before this in her letters
to the queen to "flatterers," which point at least to some suspected influence undermining her own. She tells us first in a
few succinct pages who this was whose private marriage excited so much wonder and indignation in her mind. Abigail
and all her family owed their establishment in life to the active
exertions of the duchess, who had taken them in their poverty
upon her shoulders—or rather had succeeded in passing them
on to the broader shoulders of the public, which was still more
satisfactory. Thus she had been the making of the whole band,
henceforward through other members besides Abigail to prove
thorns in her flesh. Harley, who was at this time secretary of
state, and aiming at higher place, was related in the same
degree on the father's side to Mrs. Abigail ; so that, first cousin
to the great duchess on one hand and to the leader of the
House of Commons on the other, though it suits the narrator's

purpose to humble her, Mrs. Hill was no child of the people. It is curious to remark here that Harley too came to his first advancement by Marlborough's patronage.

From the moment of this discovery, and of the further facts that the marriage had taken place under Anne's auspices, and that Abigail had already taken advantage of her favor to bring Harley into close relations with the queen, the duchess gave her mistress little peace. Fiery letters were showered daily upon the queen. She let nothing pass without a hasty visit, or a long epistle. If it were not for the pertinacity with which she returns again and again to one subject, these letters have so much force of character in them that it would be impossible not to enter with sympathetic excitement into the fray. The reader is carried along by the passionate absorption of the writer's mind as she pours forth page upon page, flying to her desk at every new incident, transmitting copies of every epistle to Godolphin to secure his coöperation, and to Marlborough, though so much farther off, to show him how she had confuted all his adversaries. And then there follows a record of stormy scenes, remonstrances, and appeals that lose their effect by repetition. The duchess would never accept defeat. Every new affront, every symptom of failure in the policy which she supported with so much zeal, made her rush, if possible, to the presence of the queen, with a storm of reproaches and invectives, with tears of fury and outcries of wrath,—or to the pen, with which she reiterated the same burning story of her wrongs. Anne is represented to us throughout in an attitude of stolid and passive resistance, which increases our sympathy with the weeping, raging, passionate woman, whose eloquence, whose arguments, whose appeals and entreaties all dash unheeded against the rock of tranquil obstinacy which is no more moved by them than the cliff is moved by the petulance of the rising tide; although, on the other hand, a similar sympathy is not

THE DUCHESS OF MARLBOROUGH.

ENGRAVED BY R. G. TIETZE, FROM MEZZOTINT AFTER PAINTING BY SIR GODFREY KNELLER.

wanting for the dull and placid soul which could get no peace, and which longed above all things for tranquillity, for gentle attentions and soft voices, and the privilege of nominating bishops and playing basset in peace. Poor lady! on the whole it is Queen Anne who is most to be pitied. She was often ill, always unwieldly and uncomfortable. She had nobody but a soft, gliding, smooth-tongued Abigail to fall back upon, while the duchess had half the great men of the time fawning upon her, putting themselves at her feet : her husband prizing a word of kindness from her more than anything in the world; her daughters describing her as the dearest mother that ever was ; money—which she loved—accumulating in her coffers ; and great Blenheim still a-building, and all kinds of noble hangings, cut velvets and satins, pictures, and every fine thing that could be conceived, getting collected for the adornment of that great house.

Nevertheless, there can be little doubt that Duchess Sarah represented a nobler idea and grander national policy than that into which her mistress was betrayed. Her later intercourse with Anne was little more than a persecution ; and yet what she aimed at was better than the dishonoring and selfish policy by which she was finally conquered. The Marlboroughs were not of those who pressed the German heir upon the queen, or would have compelled her to receive his visit, which she passionately declared she could not bear; but they were determined, all treasonable correspondence notwithstanding, upon the maintenance of the Protestant succession, upon the firm establishment of English independence and greatness,—those objects which alone had justified the Revolution and made the stern chapter of William's life and reign anything better than an incidental episode. Though he had been false to William, as everybody was false in those days, and had lain so long in the cold shade of his displeasure, Marlborough had, in his whole magnificent career, been little more than the executor of William's plans, the fulfiller of his policy. The duchess, on her side, with much love of power and of gain, with all the drawbacks of her temper and pertinacity, still bent every faculty to the work of backing up that policy, as embodied in her husband, keeping his friends in power, neutralizing the efforts of his enemies, and bringing the war to an entirely successful conclusion. A certain enlightenment was in all her passionate interferences with the course of public affairs. The men whom she labored to thrust into office were the best men of the time; the ascendency she endeavored so violently to retain was one under which England had been elevated in the scale of nations and all her liberties confirmed. Such persecuting and intolerant acts as the bill against occasional conformity, which was a test of exceptional severity, had her strenuous opposition. In short, had there been no Marlborough to carry on the half-begun war at William's death, and no Sarah at Anne's ear to inspire the queen's sluggish nature with spirit and to keep her up to the mark of the large plans of her predecessor, England might have fallen into another driveling period of foreign subserviency, into a new and meaner Restoration.

That the reader may see, however, to what an extraordinary pass the friendship had come which had been so intimate and close, we add the duchess's account of the concluding interview. Every kind of exasperating circumstance had accumulated in the mean time between the former friends. There had been violent meetings, violent letters by the score; even in the midst of a thanksgiving service Sarah had taken her mistress to task and imperiously bidden her not to answer. Indeed, the poor queen was more or less hunted down, pursued to her last corner of defense, when the mistress of the robes made her sudden appearance at Kensington one April afternoon in the year 1710, when everything was tending toward her downfall.

As I was entering, the Queen said she was just going to write to me, and when I began to speak she interrupted me four or five times with these repeated words, "Whatever you have to say you may put it in writing." I said her Majesty never did so hard a thing to any as to refuse to hear them speak, and assured her that I was not going to trouble her upon the subject which I knew to be so ungrateful to her, but that I could not possibly rest until I had cleared myself from some particular calumnies with which I had been loaded. I then went on to speak (though the Queen turned away her face from me) and to represent my hard case, that there were those about her Majesty that had made her believe that I said things of her which I was no more capable of saying than of killing my own children. The Queen said without doubt there were many lies told. I then begged, in order to make this trouble the shorter and my own innocence the plainer, that I might know the particulars of which I had been accused, because if I were guilty that would quickly appear, and if I were innocent this method alone would clear me. The Queen replied that she would give me no answer, laying hold on a word in my letter that what I had to say in my own vindication *need have no consequence in obliging her Majesty to answer*, etc., which surely did not at all imply that I did not desire to know the particular things laid to my charge, without which it was impossible for me to clear myself. This I assured her Majesty was all I desired, and that I did not ask the names of the authors or relaters of these calumnies, saying all that I could think reasonably to enforce my just request. I protested to her Majesty that I had no design in giving her this trouble, to solicit the return of her favor, but that my sole view was to clear myself: which was too just a design to be wholly disappointed by her Majesty. Upon this the Queen offered to go out of the room, I following her, and begging leave to clear myself, and the Queen repeating over and over again, "You desired no answer and shall have none." When she came to the door I fell into great disorder; streams of tears flow'd down against my will and prevented my speaking for some time. At length I recovered myself and appealed to the Queen in the vehemence of my concern whether I might not still have been happy in her Majesty's favour if I could have contradicted or dissembled my real opinion of men or things? whether I had ever, during our long friendship, told her one lie, or play'd the hypocrite once? whether I had offended in anything, unless in a very zealous pressing upon her that which I thought necessary for her service and security? I then said I was informed by a very reasonable and credible person about the court that things were laid to my charge of which I was wholly incapable; that this person knew that such stories were perpetually told to her Majesty to incense her, and had beg'd of me to come and vindicate myself: that the same person had thought me of late guilty of some omissions towards her Majesty, being entirely ignorant how uneasy to her my frequent attendance must be after what had happened between us. I explained some things which I had heard her Majesty had taken amiss of me, and then, with a fresh flood of tears and a concern sufficient to move compassion, even where all love was absent, I beg'd to know what other particulars she had heard of me, that I might not be denied all power of justifying my-self. But the only return was, "You desired no answer and you shall have none." I then beg'd to know if her Majesty would tell me some other time? "You desired no answer and you shall have none." I then appealed to her Majesty again, if she did not herself know that I had often despised interest in comparison of serving her faithfully and doing right? And whether she did not know me to be of a temper in-capable of disowning anything which I knew to be true? "You desired no answer and you shall have none." This usage was so severe, and these words, so often repeated, were so shocking (being an utter denial of common justice to one who had been a most faithful servant, and now asked nothing more) that I could not conquer myself, but said the most disrespectful thing I ever spoke to the Queen in my life, and yet what such an occasion and such circumstances might well excuse if not justify, and that was, that "I was confident her Majesty would suffer for such an instance of inhumanity." The Queen answered, "That will be to myself." Thus ended this remarkable conversation, the last I ever had with her Majesty [the duchess adds].

After this there was no more possibility of reconciliation. Attempts of all kinds were made, and there is even a record of a somewhat pitiful scene in which great Marlborough himself, on his return from the wars, appears on his knees pleading with Queen Anne to take back her old companion into favor, but without ef-fect. Unfortunately for himself, he did not resign at this turning-point, being persuaded both by friends and foes not to do so; and with the evident risk before his eyes of hazarding all the combinations of the war and giving a distinct advantage to the

enemy against whom he had hitherto operated so forcibly.   He
kept his command, therefore, for the public interest rather than
his own, and returned, when the season of warfare recom-
menced, to the post which all these events made uneasy for him,
and where his credit was shaken and his prestige diminished
by the disfavor of the court and the opposition of the ministry.
The responsibility was therefore left upon Anne and her ministers of dismissing him, which they did in the end of 1711, to the
consternation of their allies, the delight of the French, and the
bewilderment of the nation.   The party plots by which this
came about are far too long and involved to be capable of explanation here—neither can we enter into the semi-secret
negotiations for the humiliating and disgraceful peace secured
by the treaty of Utrecht, which were carried on unknown to
Marlborough, to the destruction of the alliance and confusion of
all his plans.   Never, perhaps, was so great a man treated with
such contumely.   His associate in his work, the Lord Treasurer
Godolphin, the great financier of his time, had already fallen,
leaving office so poor a man that he would have been wholly
dependent on his relations but for the unexpected death of a
brother who left him a small fortune.   He has left an account
of his dismissal by the queen herself and on the ground apparently of personal offense, which is extraordinary indeed.

Anne herself was no doubt little more than a puppet in the
hands of successive politicians; but yet the struggle that took
place around her at this unfortunate period — the maintenance
by every wile of somebody who could influence her, the conflict
for her ear and favor — shows her immense importance in the
economy of public life.   Queen Victoria is the object of universal veneration and respect, but not the smallest official in her
government need fear the displeasure of the queen as the highest minister had to fear that of Anne, for whom no one entertained any particular respect.   Yet there was little real power

in the possession of the unfortunate woman who, badgered on all sides, and refused both peace and rest, sank slowly into disease and decay during the two years which followed the disgrace of the friend of her youth.

She had no longer an audacious Freeman to tell her unwelcome truths and tease her with appeals and reproaches; but it is probable that she soon found her soft-voiced Abigail, her caressing duchess (of Somerset) little more satisfactory; never was a head that wore a crown more uneasy. She held fast to the power which she had been persuaded she was to get into her own hands when she was delivered from the sway of the Marlboroughs, and for a little while believed it possible that she could reign unaided. But this was a delusion that could not last long; and her death was hastened, it is said, by a violent altercation between Harley and St. John, when the inevitable struggle between the two who had pushed all competitors out of place occurred at last. They wrangled over the staff of office in Anne's very presence, overwhelming her with agitation and excitement. Apart from politics, the royal existence was dull enough. When Dean Swift was at Windsor, following Harley and waiting for the decision of his Irish business, we have occasional glimpses through his eyes which show the tedium of the court. "There was a drawing-room to-day," he says, "but so few company that the Queen sent for us into her bedchamber, where we made our bows, and stood, about twenty of us round the room, while she looked round with her fan in her mouth, and once a minute said about three words to some that were nearest her, and then she was told dinner was ready, and went out." The same authority mentions her way of taking exercise, which was a strange one. "The Queen was hunting the stag till four this afternoon," he says; "she drove in her chaise about forty miles, and it was five before we went to dinner. . . . She hunts in a chaise with one horse, which she drives herself, and drives furiously like Jehu, and is a mighty hunter like Nimrod." Windsor's great park and forest must have afforded room and space for some part at least of this course, and a hunt in August would need to have been confined to ground less cultivated than that of the smiling plain which skirts the castle hill on the other side. Queen Anne's Ride and Queen Anne's Drive are still well-known names in the locality where the strange apparition of the queen, solitary in her high chaise, and "driving furiously" after the hunt must once have been a familiar sight.

The end of this poor queen's life was disturbed by a new and terrible struggle, in which natural sentiment and public duty, and all the prepossessions and prejudices of her nature, were set in conflict one against the other. This was upon the question of the succession. The family of Hanover, the Electress Sophia and her son and grandson, had been chosen solemnly by Parliament as the nearest members of the royal race who were Protestants, and were recognized as the heirs to the throne in all public acts and in the prayers of the church. But to Anne the house of Hanover was of no special interest. She did not love the idea of successor at all. She had declared to Marlborough passionately that the proposed visit of the Hanoverian prince was a thing which she could not bear, and there was no friendship, nor even acquaintance, between her and relatives so far removed. But apart from all public knowledge, in the secret chambers and by the back-stairs came whispers now of another name, that of James Stuart, more familiar and kindly—the baby-brother about whom Anne had believed the prevailing fable, that he was a supposititious child, for whom she had invented the name of the Pretender, but who now in her childless decay began to be presented before her as the victim of a great wrong. Poor queen! she was torn asunder by all these contradictions; and if her heart was melt-

ing toward her father's son, all the dull experience which she
had acquired in spite of herself must have convinced her that
this solution of the difficulty was impossible.   Her life of late
had been one long conflict; imperious Sarah first, then Harley
and St. John quarrelling in her very presence-chamber; and
when the door was shut and the curtains drawn and all the
world departed save Abigail lying on a mattress on the floor to
be near her mistress, here was the most momentous question
of all.   She who desired nothing so much as quiet and to be
left in peace, was once again compelled to face a problem of
the utmost importance to England, and on which she alone had
the power to say a decisive word.   Little wonder if Anne was
harassed beyond all endurance.   But those who pressed this
question upon her waning senses were the instruments of their
own overthrow.   The powers of life worn out before their time
could bear no more.   The hopes of the Jacobite party were
rising higher every day as the end drew near; but at the last
she escaped them, having uttered no word of support to their
cause; and in the confusion which ensued, George I. was peace-
fully proclaimed as soon as the queen out of her lethargy had
slipped beyond the boundaries of any earthly kingdom.

The Marlboroughs, who had been living on the Continent
since their disgrace, came back after this new change.   The
duke's entry into London "in great state, attended by hun-
dreds of gentlemen on horseback and some of the nobility in
their coaches" a few days after, is reported by one of the
chroniclers of the time.   The duchess followed him soon after,
and whether her temper and disposition had so far mended as
to allow him to enjoy the peace he had so often longed for
by the side of her he loved, he had at least a tranquil evening-
time among his friends and dependents, and the grandchildren
who were to be his heirs — for only one of his own children
survived at his death.   Duchess Sarah lived long after him.

BISHOP GILBERT BURNET.

ENGRAVED BY R. A. MULLER, FROM MEZZOTINT IN THE BRITISH MUSEUM
BY JOHN SMITH, AFTER OIL PAINTING BY JOHN RILEY.

She was sixty-two when he died, but, nevertheless, in spite of temper and every other failing, was still charming enough to be sought in marriage by two distinguished suitors — one of them that proud Duke of Somerset whose first wife had supplanted her at court. She answered this potentate in the only way consistent with the dignity of a woman of her age and circumstances; but added, with a noble pride which sat well upon her, that had she been but half her age, not the emperor of the world should ever have filled the place sacred to great Marlborough. It is a pity we could not leave her here in the glow of this proud tenderness and constancy. She was capable of that and many other noble things, but not of holding her tongue, of withdrawing into the background, or accepting in other ways the natural change from maturity to age. Her restless energies, however, had some legitimate outlet. She finished Blenheim, and she wrote innumerable explanations and memoranda, which finally shaped themselves into that "Account of the Conduct of the Duchess of Marlborough from her first Coming to Court," which is one of the most interesting of all *mémoires pour servir*. This was published in her eighty-second year, and it is curious to think of the vivacious and unsubdued spirit which could throw itself back so completely out of the calm of age into the conflicts and the very atmosphere of what had passed thirty years before. And she did her best to prepare for a great life of Marlborough which should set him right with the world. But her time was not always so innocently employed, and it is to be feared that she wrangled to the end of her life. The " Characters " of her contemporaries which she left behind are full of spite and malice. There was no peace in her soul. A characteristic little story is told of her in an illness. " Last year she had lain a great while ill without speaking; her physicians said she must be blistered or she would die. She called out, ' I won't be blistered and I won't

6

die!' and apparently for the moment kept her word." She lived long enough to be impaled by Pope in verses which an involuntary admiration for this daring, dauntless, impassioned woman makes us reluctant to quote. She survived almost her entire generation, and was capable of living a hundred years more had nature permitted. She was eighty-four when she succumbed at last, in the year 1744, thirty years after the death of the queen.

CHAPTER III

THE AUTHOR OF "GULLIVER"

THERE are few figures in history, and still fewer in literature, which have occupied so great a place in the world's attention, or which retain so strong a hold upon its interest, as that of Jonathan Swift, dean of St. Patrick's. It is considerably more than a century since he died, old and mad and miserable: a man who had never been satisfied with life, or felt his fate equal to his deserts; who disowned and hated (even when he served it) the country of his birth, and with fierce and bitter passion denounced human nature itself, and left a sting in almost every individual whom he loved; a man whose preferment and home were far from the center of public affairs, and who had no hereditary claim on the attention of England. Yet when the English reader, or he who in the farthest corner of the New World has the same right to English literature as that which the subjects of Queen Victoria hold,— as the American does—from the subjects of Queen Anne,— reads the title at the head of this page, neither the one nor the other will have any difficulty in distinguishing among all the ecclesiastical dignitaries of that age who it is that stands conspicuous as the dean. Not in royal Westminster or Windsor is this man to be found; not the ruler of any great cathedral in the rich English midlands where tradition and wealth and an almost Catholic supremacy united to make the great official of the church as important as any official of the state—but far from those influences, half as far as America is now from the center of English society and the sources of power, one of a nation which the most obstinate conservative of to-day will not hesitate to allow was then deeply wronged and cruelly misgoverned by England, many and anxious as have been her efforts since to make amends. Yet among the many strange examples of that far more than republican power (not always most evident in republics) by which a man of native force and genius, however humble, finds his way to the head of affairs and impresses his individuality upon his age, when thousands born to better fortunes are swept away as nobodies, Swift is one of the most remarkable. His origin, though noted by himself, not without a certain pride, as from a family of gentry not unknown in their district, was in his own person almost as lowly and poor as it was possible to be. The posthumous son of a poor official in the Dublin law-courts, owing his education to the kindness, or perhaps less the kindness than the family pride, of an uncle, Swift entered the world as a hanger-on, waiting what fortune and a patron might do for him, a position scarcely comprehensible to young Englishmen nowadays, though then the natural method of advancement. Such a young man in the present day would betake himself to his books, with the practical aim of an examination before him, and the hope of immediate admission through that gate to the public service and all its chances. It is amusing to speculate what the difference might have been had Jonathan Swift, coming raw with his degree from Trinity College, Dublin, shouldered his robust way to the head of an examination list, and thus making himself at a stroke independent of patronage, gone out to reign and rule and distribute justice in India, or pushed himself upward among the gentlemanly mediocrities of a public office. One asks would he have found that method more successful, and endured the desk and the routine of his office, and

JONATHAN SWIFT.

FROM PHOTOGRAPH OF ORIGINAL MARBLE BUST OF SWIFT
BY ROUBILLIAC (1695-1762), NOW IN THE LIBRARY OF
TRINITY COLLEGE, DUBLIN.

"got on" with the head of his department, better than he
endured the monotony and subjection, the possible slights and
spurns of Sir William Temple's household, which he entered,
half servant, half equal, the poor relation, the secretary and
companion of that fastidious philosopher? The question may
be cut short by the almost certainty that Swift could not have
gained his promotion in any such way; but his age had not
learned the habit of utilizing education, and he was one of the
idle youths of fame. "He was stopped of his degree," he himself writes in his autobiographical notes, "for dullness and
insufficiency, and at last hardly admitted in a manner little to
his credit, which is called in that college *speciali gratia*." Recent biographers have striven to prove that this really meant
nothing to Swift's discredit, but it is to be supposed that in such
a matter he is himself the best authority.

The life of the household of dependents at Moor Park,
where young Swift attended Sir William's pleasure in the
library, while the Johnsons and Dingleys, the waiting-gentle-
women of a system which now lingers only in courts, hung
about my lady, her relatives, gossips, servants, is to us extremely difficult to realize, and still more to understand. This
little cluster of secondary personages, scarcely at all elevated
above the servants, with whom they sometimes sat at table, and
whose offices they were always liable to be called on to perform, yet who were all conscious of gentle blood in their veins,
and a relationship more or less distinct with the heads of the
house, is indeed one of the most curious lingerings of the past
in the eighteenth century. When we read in one of Macaulay's brilliant sketches, or in Swift's own words, or in the indi-
cations given by both history and fiction, that the parson,—
perhaps at the great house,— humble priest of the parish,
found his natural mate in the waiting-maid, it is generally forgotten that the waiting-maid was then in most cases quite as

6*

good as the parson : a gently bred and well-descended woman,
like her whom an unkind but not ignoble fate made into the
Stella we all know, the mild and modest star of Swift's existence.   It was no doubt a step in the transition from the great
medieval household, where the squire waited on the knight
with a lowliness justified by his certainty of believing himself
knight in his turn, and where my lady's service was a noble
education, the only school accessible to the young gentlewomen
of her connection — down to our own less picturesque and
more independent days, in which personal service has ceased
to be compatible with the pretensions of any who can assume,
by the most distant claim, to be "gentle" folk.   The institution is very apparent in Shakspere's day, the waiting-gentle-
women who surround his heroines being of entirely different
mettle from the soubrettes of modern comedy.   At a later
period such a fine gentleman as John Evelyn, in no need of
patronage, was content and proud that his daughter should
enter a great household to learn how to comport herself in the
world.   In the end of the seventeenth century the dependents
were perhaps more absolutely dependent.   But even this, like
most things, had its better and worst side.

    That a poor widow with her child, like Stella's mother,
should find refuge in the house of her wealthy kinswoman at no
heavier cost than that of attending to Lady Temple's linen and
laces, and secure thus such a training for her little girl as might
indeed have ended in the rude household of a Parson Trulliber,
but at the same time might fit her to take her place in a witty
and brilliant society, and enter into all the thoughts of the most
brilliant genius of his time, was no ill fate ; nor is there anything that is less than noble and befitting (in theory) in the
association of that young man of genius, whatsoever exercises
of patience he might be put to, with the highly cultured man of
the world, the ex-ambassador and councilor of kings, under

whose auspices he could learn to understand both books and
men, see the best company of his time, and acquire at second
hand all the fruits of a ripe experience. So that, perhaps,
there is something to be said after all for the curious little community at Moor Park, where Sir William, like a god, made the
day good or evil for his people according as he smiled or
frowned; where the young Irish secretary, looking but uneasily
upon a world in which his future fate was so unassured, had
yet the wonderful chance once, if no more, of explaining English institutions to King William, and in his leisure the amusement of teaching little Hester how to write, and learning from
her baby prattle — which must have been the delight of the
house, kept up and encouraged by her elders — that "little
language" which had become a sort of synonym for the most
intimate and endearing utterances of tenderness. No doubt
Sir William himself (who left her a modest little fortune when
he died) must have loved to hear the child talk, and even Lady
Giffard and the rest, having no responsibility for her parts
of speech, kept her a baby as long as possible, and delighted
in the pretty jargon to which foolish child-lovers cling in all
ages after the little ones themselves are grown too wise to
use it more.

Jonathan Swift left Ireland, along with many more, in the
commotion that succeeded the revolution of 1688 — a very poor
and homely lad, with nothing but the learning, such as it was,
picked up in a somewhat disorderly university career. Through
his mother, then living at Leicester, and on the score of humble relationship between Mrs. Swift and Lady Temple, of whom
the reader may perhaps remember the romance and tender history,—a pleasant association,— he was introduced to Sir William Temple's household, but scarcely, it would appear, at first
to any permanent position there. He was engaged, an un-
friendly writer says, "at the rate of £20 a year" as amanuensis

and reader, but "Sir William never favoured him with his conversation nor allowed him to sit at table with him." Temple's
own account of the position, however, contains nothing at all
derogatory to the young man, for whom, about a year after,
he endeavored, no doubt in accordance with Swift's own wishes,
to find a situation with Sir Robert Southwell, then going to
Ireland as secretary of state. Sir William describes Swift as "of
good family in Herefordshire. . . . He has lived in my house,
read to me, writ for me, and kept all my accounts as far as my
small occasions required. He has Latin and Greek, some
French, writes a very good current hand, is very honest and
diligent, and has good friends, though they have for the present
lost their fortunes," the great man says; and he recommends
the youth "either as a gentleman to wait on you, or a clerk to
write under you, or upon any establishment of the College to
recommend him to a fellowship there, which he has a just pretence to." This shows how little there was in the position of
"a gentleman to wait on you," of which the young suitor need
have been ashamed. Swift's own account of this speedy return to Ireland is that it was by advice of the physicians,
"who weakly imagined that his native air might be of some use
to recover his health," which he was young enough to have
endangered by the temptations of Sir William's fine gardens;
a "surfeit of fruit" being the innocent cause to which he
attributes the disease which haunted him for all the rest of
his life.

His absence, however, from the Temple household was of
very short duration, Sir Robert Southwell having apparently
had no use for his services, or means of preferring him to a fellowship, and he returned to Moor Park in 1690, where he remained for four years. It was quite clear, whatever his vicis-
situdes of feeling might have been, that he identified himself
entirely with his patron's opinions and even prejudices, and was

MOOR PARK, RESIDENCE OF SIR WILLIAM TEMPLE,
AND OF SWIFT.

DRAWN BY CHARLES HERBERT WOODBURY. ENGRAVED BY R. VARLEY.

a loyal and devoted retainer both now and afterward. When
Sir William became involved in a literary quarrel with the
great scholar Bentley, young Swift rushed into the field with a
jeu d'esprit which has outlived all other records of the controversy. The "Battle of the Books" could hardly have been
written in aid of a hard or contemptuous master. Years after,
when he had a house of his own and had entered upon his independent career, he turned his little rectory garden into a
humble imitation of the Dutch paradise which Temple had
made to bloom in the wilds of Surrey, with a canal and a wil-
low walk like those which were so dear to King William and
his courtiers. And when Temple died, it was to Swift, and
not to any of his nephews, that Sir William committed the
charge of his papers and literary remains. This does not look
like a hard bondage on one side, or any tyrannical sway on the
other, notwithstanding a few often-quoted phrases which are
taken as implying complaint. "Don't you remember," Swift
asks long after, "how I used to be in pain when Sir William
Temple would look cold and out of temper for three or four
days, and I used to suspect a hundred reasons?" But these
words need not represent anything more than that sensitiveness
to the aspect of the person on whom his prospects and comfort
depend which is inevitable to every individual in a similar position, however considerate and friendly the patron may be. The
hard-headed and unbending Scotch philosopher, James Mill,
was just as sensitive to the looks of his kind friend and helper
in the early struggles of life, Jeremy Bentham, in whose sunny
countenance Mill discovered unspoken offense with an ingenuity worthy of a self-tormenting woman. It was natural indeed
that Swift, a high-spirited young man, should fret and struggle
as the years went on and nothing happened to enlarge his
horizon beyond the trees of Moor Park. He was sent to King
William, as has been said when Temple was unable to wait

upon his Majesty, to explain to him the expediency of certain
parliamentary measures, and this was no doubt intended by his
patron as a means of bringing him under the king's notice.
William would seem to have taken a kind of vague interest in
the secretary, which he expressed in an odd way by offering
him a captain's commission in a cavalry regiment,—a proposal
which did not tempt Swift,—and by teaching him how to cut
asparagus "in the Dutch way," and to eat up all the stalks, as
the dean afterward, in humorous revenge, made an unlucky
visitor of his own do.   But William, notwithstanding these
whimsical evidences of favor, neither listened to the young secretary's argument nor gave him a prebend as had been hoped.

Four years, however, is a long time for an ambitious young
man to spend in dependence, watching one hope die out after
another; and Swift's impatience began to be irrestrainable and
to trouble the peace of his patron's learned leisure.   Although
destined from the first to the church, and for some time waiting
in tremulous expectation of ecclesiastical preferment, Swift had
not yet taken orders.   The explanation he gives of how and
why he finally determined on doing so is characteristic.   His
dissatisfaction and restlessness, probably his complaints, moved
Sir William,—though evidently deeply offended that his secretary should wish to leave him,—to offer him an employ of
about £120 a year in the Rolls Office in Ireland, of which
Temple held the sinecure office of master.   "Whereupon [says
Swift's own narrative] Mr. Swift told him that since he had now
an opportunity of living without being driven into the Church
for a maintenance, he was resolved to go to Ireland and take
Holy Orders."   This arbitrary decision to balk his patron's
tardy bounty, and take his own way in spite of him, was probably as much owing to a characteristic blaze of temper as to the
somewhat fantastic disinterestedness here put forward, though
Swift was never a man greedy of money or disposed to sacrifice

his pride to the acquisition of gain, notwithstanding certain habits of miserliness afterward developed in his character. Sir William was "extremely angry"—hurt, no doubt, as many a patron has been, by the ingratitude of the dependent who would not trust everything to him, but claimed some free will in the disposition of his own life. Had they been uncle and nephew, or even father and son, the same thing might easily have happened. Swift set out for Dublin full of indignation and excitement, "everybody judging I did best to leave him,"—but alas! in this, as in so many cases, pride was doomed to speedy downfall.

On reaching Dublin, and taking the necessary steps for his ordination, Swift found that it was needful for him to have a recommendation and certificate from the patron in whose house so many years of his life had been spent. No doubt it must have been a somewhat bitter necessity to bow his head before the protector whom he had left in anger and ask for this. Macaulay describes him as addressing his patron in the language "of a lacquey, or even of a beggar," but we doubt greatly if apart from prejudice or the tingle of these unforgettable words, any impartial reader would form such an impression. "The particulars expected of me," Swift writes, "are what relates to morals and learning and the reasons of quitting your honour's family, that is whether the last was occasioned by any ill action." "Your honour" has a somewhat servile tone in our days, but in Swift's the formality was natural. Lady Giffard, Temple's sister-in-law, in the further quarrels which followed Sir William's death, spoke of this as a penitential letter, and perhaps it was not wonderful that she should look on the whole matter with an unfavorable eye. No doubt the ladies of the house thought young Swift an unnatural monster for wishing to go away and thinking himself able to set up for himself without their condescending notice and the godlike philosopher's

society and instruction, and were pleased to find his pride so
quickly brought down. Sir William, however, it would seem,
behaved as a philosopher and a gentleman should, and gave
the required recommendation with magnanimity and kindness.
Thus the young man had his way.

Swift got a small benefice in the north of Ireland, the little
country parish of Kilroot, in which doubtless he expected that
the sense of independence would make up to him for other
deprivations. It was near Belfast, among those hard-headed
Scotch colonists whom he could never endure; and probably
this had something to do with the speedy revulsion of his mind.
He remained there only a year; and it is perhaps the best
proof we could have of his sense of isolation and banishment
that this was the only time in his life in which he thought of
marriage. There is in existence a fervent and impassioned letter addressed to the object of his affections, a Miss Waring,
whom, after the fashion of the time, he called Varina. He does
not seem in this case to have had the usual good fortune that
attended his relationships with women. Miss Waring did not respond with the same warmth; indeed, she was discouraging and
coldly prudent. And he was still pleading for a favorable answer
when there arrived a letter from Moor Park inviting his return
— Sir William's pride, too, having apparently broken down
under the blank made by Swift's departure. He made instant
use of this invitation — which must have soothed his injured
feelings and restored his self-satisfaction — to shake the resolution of the ungrateful Varina. " I am once more offered," he says,
"the advantage to have the same acquaintance with greatness
which I formerly enjoyed, and with better prospects of interest";
and though he offers magnanimously "to forego it all for your
sake," yet it is evident that the proposal had set the blood stirring in his veins, and that the dependence from which he had
broken loose with a kind of desperation, once more seemed to

DEAN SWIFT.

FROM COPPERPLATE ENGRAVING BY PIERRE FOURDRINIER,
AFTER A PAINTING BY CHARLES JERVAS.

him, unless Varina had been melted by the sacrifice he would have made for her, to be the most desirable thing in the world.

Macaulay, and after him Thackeray and many less distinguished writers, still persistently represent this part of Swift's life as one of unmitigated hardship and suffering. The brilliant historian so much scorns the guidance of facts as to say that the humble student "made love to a pretty waiting-maid who was the chief ornament of the servant's hall," by way of explaining the strange yet tender story which has been more deeply discussed than any great national event, and which has made the name of Stella known to every reader.

Hester Johnson was a child of seven when young Swift, "the humble student," went first to Moor Park. She was only fifteen when he returned, no longer as a sort of educated man of all work, but on the entreaty of the patron who had felt the want of his company so much as to forget all grievances. He was not now a humble student, Temple's satellite and servant, but his friend and coadjutor, fully versed in all his secrets, and most likely already chosen as the guardian of his fame and the executor of his purposes and wishes; therefore it is not possible that Macaulay's reckless picturesque description could apply to either time. Such an easy picture, however, has more effect upon the general imagination than the outcries of all the biographers, and the many researches made to show that Swift was not a sort of literary lackey, nor Stella an Abigail, but that he had learned to prize the advantages of his home there during his absence from it, and that during the latter part of his life at Moor Park at least his position was as good as that of a dependent can ever be.

Sir William Temple died, as Swift records affectionately, on the morning of January 27, 1699, "and with him all that was good and amiable among men." He died, however, leaving the young man who had spent so many years of his life under

his wing, scarcely better for that long subjection.   Swift had a
legacy of £100 for his trouble in editing his patron's memoirs,
and he got the profits of those memoirs, amounting, Mr. Forster calculates, to no less than £600 — no inconsiderable present; but no one of the many appointments which were then
open to the retainers of the great, and especially to a young
man of letters, had come in Swift's way.   He himself, it is
said, "still believed in the royal pledge for the first prebend
that should fall vacant in Westminster or Canterbury," but this
was a hope which had accompanied him ever since he explained constitutional law to King William six years before,
and could not be very lively after this long interval.

Thus Swift's life came to a sudden and complete break.
The great household, with its easy and uneasy jumble of patrons
and dependents, fell asunder and ceased to be.   The younger
members of the family were jealous of the last bequest, which
put the fame of their distinguished relative into the hands of a
stranger, and did their best to set Swift down in his proper place,
and to proclaim how much he was the creature of their uncle's
bounty.   In the breaking up which followed, there were many
curious partings and conjunctions.   Why Hester Johnson, to
whom Sir William had bequeathed a little independence, should
have left her mother's care and joined her fortunes to those of
Mrs. Dingley instead, remains unexplained, unless indeed it was
Mrs. Johnson's second marriage which was the cause, or perhaps
some vexation on the part of Lady Giffard—with whom the
girl's mother remained, notwithstanding her marriage—at the
liberality of her brother to the child brought up in his house.
Mrs. Johnson had other daughters, one of whom Swift saw, and
describes favorably, years after.   Perhaps Mrs. Dingley and the
girl whom he had taught and petted from her childhood had
taken Swift's side in the Giffard-Temple difference, and so got
on uneasy terms with the rest of the household, always faithful

to my lady. At all events, at the breaking up Hester with her little fortune separated herself from the connection generally, and with her elder friend made an independent new beginning, as Swift also had to do. The fact seems of no particular importance, except that it afforded a reason for Swift's interference in her affairs, and threw them into a combination which lasted all their lives.

Swift was thirty-one, too old to be beginning his career, yet young enough to turn with eager zest to the unknown, when this catastrophe occurred. Sir William Temple's secretary and literary executor must have known, one would suppose, many people who could have helped him to promotion, but it would seem as if a kind of irresistible fate impelled him back to his native country, though he did not love it, and forced him to be an Irishman in spite of himself. The only post that came in his way was a chaplaincy, conjoined with a secretaryship, in the suite of the Earl of Berkeley, newly appointed one of the lords justices in Ireland, and just then entering upon his duties. Swift accepted the position in hopes that he should be continued as Lord Berkeley's secretary, and possibly go with him afterward to more stirring scenes and a larger life, but this expectation was not carried out. Neither was his application — which seems at the moment a somewhat bold one — for the deanery of Derry successful, and all the preferment he succeeded in getting was another Irish living, with a better stipend and in a more favorable position than Kilroot: the parish of Laracor, within twenty miles of Dublin, which, conjoined with a prebend in St. Patrick's and other small additions, brought him in £200 a year; a small promotion, indeed, yet not a bad income for the place and time. And he was naturally, as Lord Berkeley's chaplain, in the midst of the finest company that Ireland could boast, one of a court more extended than Sir William Temple's, yet of a similar description, and affording greater scope for his

hitherto undeveloped social qualities. Satire more sportive
than mere scorn, yet sometimes savage enough ; an elephantine
fun, which pleased the age ; the puns and quibs in which the
men emulated one another ; the merry rhymes that pleased the
ladies,—seem suddenly to have burst forth in him, throwing an
unexpected gleam upon his new sphere.

Swift was always popular with women. He treated them
roughly on many occasions, with an arrogance that grew with
age, but evidently possessed that charm—a quality by itself and
not dependent upon any laws of amiability—which attracts one
sex to the other. Lady Berkeley, whom he describes as a woman of "the most easy conversation joined with the truest
piety," and her young daughters were charming and lively
companions with whom the chaplain soon found himself at
home. And notwithstanding his disappointment with respect
to the preferment which Lord Berkeley might have procured
for him and did not, it would seem that this period of hanging
on at the little Irish court was amusing at least. The lively
little picture of the inferior members of a great household which
Swift made for the entertainment of the drawing-rooms on the
occasion when Mrs. Frances Harris lost her purse, is one of the
most vivid and amusing possible.

His stay in Ireland at this period lasted about two years,
during which he paid repeated visits to his living at Laracor,
and made trial of existence there also. The parsonage was in
a ruinous condition ; the church a miserable barn ; the congrega-
tion numbered about twenty persons. Many are the tales of
the new parson's arrival there like a thunder-storm, frightening
the humble curate and his wife with the arrogant roughness of
manner which they, like many others, found afterward covered
a great deal of genuine practical kindness. His mode of travel-
ing, his sarcastic rhymes about the places at which he paused
on the journey, the careless swing of imperious good and ill

STELLA'S COTTAGE, ON THE BOUNDARY OF
THE MOOR PARK ESTATE.

DRAWN BY CHARLES HERBERT WOODBURY.
ENGRAVED BY S. DAVIS.

humor in which he indulged, contemptuous of everybody's
opinion, have furnished many amusing incidents. One well-
known anecdote, which describes him as finding his congrega-
tion to consist only of his clerk and beginning the service
gravely with, " Dearly beloved Roger," has found a permanent
place among ecclesiastical pleasantries. In all probability it is
true ; but if not so, it is at least so *ben trovato* as to be as good
as true. There were few claims upon the energies of such a
man in such a sphere, and when Lord Berkeley was recalled to
England his chaplain went with him. But neither did he find
any promotion in London. Up to this time his only literary
work had been that wonderful "Battle of the Books," which
had burst like a bombshell into the midst of the squabble of the
literati, but which had only as yet been handed about in manuscript, and was therefore known to few. No doubt it was
known to various wits and scholars that Sir William Temple's
late secretary and literary executor was a young man of no
common promise; but statesmen in general, and the king in
particular, sick and worn out with many preoccupations, had
no leisure for the claims of the Irish parson. He hung about
the Berkeley household, and gravely read out of the book of
moral essays which the countess loved those Reflections on a
Broomstick which her ladyship found so edifying, and launched
upon the world an anonymous pamphlet or two, which he had
the pleasure of hearing talked about and attributed to names
greater than his own, but made no step toward the advancement for which he longed.

The interest of this visit to England was however as great
and told for as much in his life as if it had brought him a
bishopric. It determined that long connection and close intercourse in which Swift's inner history is involved. After he had
paid in vain his court to the king, and made various ineffectual
attempts to recommend himself in high quarters, he went on a

7

visit to Farnham, where Hester Johnson and Mrs. Dingley had settled after Sir William's death.   Swift found the two women quite undetermined what to do, in an uncomfortable lodging, harassed for money, and without any object in their lives.   Most probably he was called to advise as to their future plans, where they should settle and how they were to live, both being entirely inexperienced in the art of independent existence.   They had lived together for years, and knew everything about each other : Hester had grown up from childhood under Swift's eye, his pupil, his favorite and playfellow.   She had now, it is true, arrived at an age when other sentiments are supposed to come in.   She must have been about twenty, while he was thirty-four.   There was no reason in the world why they should not have married then and there, had they so wished.   But there seems no appearance or thought of any such desire, and the question was what should the ladies do for the arrangement of their affairs and pleasant occupation of their lives.   Farnham being untenable, where should they go?   Why not to Ireland, where Hester's property was—where they would be near their friend, who could help them into society and give them his own companionship as often as he happened to be there?   Here is his own account of the decision:

"I prevailed with her and her dear friend and companion, the other lady," he says, "to draw what money they had into Ireland, a great part of their fortunes being in annuities upon funds.   Money was then ten per cent. in Ireland, besides the advantage of returning it, and all the necessaries of life at half the price.   They complied with my advice, and soon after came over ; but I happening to continue some time longer in England, they were much discouraged to live in Dublin, where they were wholly strangers.   But this adventure looked so like a frolic, the censure held for some time as if there were a secret history in such a removal ; which however soon blew off by her excellent conduct. She came over with her friend in the year 1700, and they both lived together until the day [of her death, 1728]."

This was then the time which decided that which is called the "sad and mysterious history" of Swift and Stella—a story so strangely told, so obstinately insisted upon as miserable, unnatural, and tragical, that the reader or writer of to-day has scarcely the power of forming an impartial judgment upon it. We have not a word from the woman's side of the question, who is supposed to have passed a melancholy existence of unsatisfied longings and disappointed love by Swift's side, the victim of his capricious affections, neglect, cruelty, and fondness. That she should have wished to marry him, that the love was impassioned on her side, and her whole life blighted and overcast by his fantastic repugnance to the common ties of humanity, is taken for granted by every historian. These writers differ as to Swift's motives, as to the character of his feelings, and even as to the facts of the case; but no one has the slightest doubt of what the woman's sentiments must have been. But, as a matter of fact, we have no evidence at all what Stella's sentiments were. By so much written testimony as remains we are fully entitled to form such conclusions as we please on Swift's side of the question; but there is actually no testimony at all upon Stella's side. Appearances of blighted life or unhappiness there are none in anything we know of her. As the ladies appear reflected in that "Journal to Stella"—which is the dean's only claim upon our affections, but a strong one —they seem to have lived a most cheerful, lively life. They had a number of friends, they had their little tea-parties, their circle of witty society, to which the letters of the absent were a continual amusement and delight. And it is the man, not the woman, who complains of not receiving letters; it is he, not she, who exhausts every playful wile, every tender art, to keep himself in vivid recollection. Is it perhaps a certain mixture of masculine vanity and compassion for the gentle feminine creature who never succeeded in getting the man she loved to marry her, and thus failed to attain the highest end of woman, which has moved every biographer of Swift, each man more compassionate than his predecessor, thus to exhaust himself in pity for Stella? Johnson, Scott, Macaulay, Thackeray, not to mention many lesser names, have all taken her injured innocence to heart. And nobody notes the curious fact that Stella herself never utters any complaint, nor indeed seems to feel the necessity of being unhappy at all, but takes her dean most cheerfully,—laughing, scolding, giving her opinion with all the delightful freedom of a relationship which was at once nature and choice, the familiar trust and tenderness of old use and wont with the charm of voluntary association. We see her only as reflected in his letters, in the references he makes to hers, and all his tender, sportive allusions to her habits and ways of thinking. This reflection and image is not in rigid lines of black and white, but an airy and radiant vision, the representation of anything in the world rather than a downcast and disappointed woman. It is not that either of a wife or a lover; it is more like the wilful, delightful image of a favorite child, a creature confident that everything she says or does will be received with admiration from the mere fact that it is she who says or does it, and who tyrannizes, scoffs, and proffers a thousand comments and criticisms with all the elastic brightness of unforced and unimpassioned affection. It is through this medium alone that Stella is ever visible. And he, too, laughs, teases, fondles, and advises with the same doting, delightful ease of affection. By what process this attractive conjunction should have furnished the idea of a victim in Stella, and in Swift of a tyrannous secret lover crushing her heart, it is difficult to understand. The external circumstances of their intimacy were, no doubt, very

HESTER JOHNSON, SWIFT'S "STELLA," PAINTED FROM LIFE
BY MRS. DELANY, ON THE WALL OF THE TEMPLE
AT DELVILLE, AND ACCIDENTALLY DESTROYED.

ENGRAVED BY M. HAIDER, FROM COPY OF THE ORIGINAL BY HENRY MACMANUS,
R. H. A., NOW IN POSSESSION OF PROFESSOR DOWDEN.

unusual, and might have lent occasion to much evil speaking. But they do not seem to have done so, after the first moment at least. Nobody ventured to assail the good fame of Stella, and Swift took every means to make the perfect innocence of their friendship apparent. She cannot be made out to have suffered in the vulgar way, and it seems to us one of the most curious examples of an obstinately maintained theory to represent her as Swift's victim in what is supposed to be a long martyrdom of the heart.

One can well imagine, however, when the two ladies arrived in Dublin, where their friend had no doubt represented to them his power to gain them access into the best society, and found that he did not come and that they were stranded in a strange place, knowing nobody, how some annoyance and disappointment, and perhaps anger, must have been in their thoughts, and that P. D. F. R., as he is called in the little language, faithless rogue! had his share of abuse. And no doubt it might be believed by good-natured friends that their object in coming was to secure the vicar of Laracor either for the young and lovely girl or the elder woman, who was scarcely older than Swift—if not indeed that some "secret history" more damaging still was at the bottom of the adventure. Insensibly, however, Mrs. Johnson and Mrs. Dingley found a place and position for themselves. Swift was often away in the following years, spending about half his time in London, and when he was absent they took possession of his newly repaired and renovated house; or occupied his lodging in Dublin, and gathered friends about them, and went out to their card-parties, and played a little, and talked, and lived a pleasant life. When he returned, they removed to their own rooms. Thus there could be no doubt about the close association between them, which, when it was quite apparent that it meant nothing closer to come, no doubt made everybody wonder. But we have no con-

7*

temporary evidence that Stella was an object of pity, and her aspect as we see it in all Swift says of her is exactly the reverse, and gives us the impression of a charming and easy-minded woman, a queen of society in her little circle, enjoying everything that came her way.

As Swift's relations with Stella are the great interests of his life, the subject which occupies every new writer who so much as touches upon him, it is needless to make any excuse for entering into the question with an amount of detail which our limited space would otherwise scarcely justify. The mystery about it lends it an endless attraction, and as, whatever it was, it is the one great love of his life, and represents all the private satisfaction and comfort he got by means of his affections, it has a permanent interest which most readers will not find in the "Tale of a Tub," or any other of the productions which made this period of his life remarkable. Swift was continually going and coming to London through these years. Though he had begun at once to make Laracor a sort of earthly paradise with a Dutch flavor, such as he had learnt from his early master, and though it was "very much for his own satisfaction" that he had invited Stella to come to Ireland, yet neither of these reasons was enough to keep him in the rural quiet among his willows, though he loved them. He hankered after society, after fame and power. He liked to meet with great men, to hear the news, to ride over weaker reasoners in society, to put forth his own vigorous views, and whip, with sharp satire, the men who displeased him. Tradition and habit had made him a Whig, but political names were of easy interchange in those days, and Swift's objects were much more definite than his politics. From the moment of Queen Anne's ascension, when she gratified the Church of England by the remission of certain dues hitherto paid to the crown, Swift's energies were directed to obtaining a similar remission for the Irish Church, and this was the ostensible object of his repeated journeys to London. He had also a purpose still nearer to his heart, which was the advancement of Jonathan Swift to a post more fitted to his genius. For these great objects he haunted the anterooms of Halifax and Somers and Godolphin, and did what he could to show them what they were not wise enough to perceive, that he was himself an auxiliary well worth securing. The Whig lords played with, flattered, and neglected the brilliant but importunate envoy of the Irish Church, holding him upon tenterhooks of expectation, going so far as to make him believe that his cause for the church was won, and that his bishopric was certain, till disgust and disappointment overcame Swift's patience. Nine years had passed in these vain negotiations. It was in 1701 that he paid that visit to Farnham which decided Stella's fate, but his own was still hanging in the balance when after almost yearly expeditions in the interval, he set out for London in the autumn of the year 1710 with a threat upon his lips. "I will apply to Mr. Harley, who formerly made some advances toward me, and, unless he be altered, will I believe think himself in the right to use me well." The change was sudden, but it had little in it that could be called political apostasy. Every man was more or less for his own hand, and the balance of popular feeling fluctuated between war and peace: between pride and the glory of England on the one hand, and horror of the sacrifices and misery involved in the long-continued, never-ending campaigns of Marlborough on the other—almost as much as Queen Anne wavered between the influence of the imperious duchess and the obsequious Abigail. There was no shame to Swift at such a moment in the sudden revolution he made.

The man who felt himself of sufficient importance to make this threat seems to have possessed already, notwithstanding the neglect of the Whig lords, the rank of his intellect rather than of his external position, and this not entirely because of the anonymous productions which were more or less known to be his. The "Tale of a Tub," written while he was still an inmate of Moor Park, had by this time been before the world six years. It was published along with the "Battle of the Books" in 1704, and caused great excitement and sensation among politicians, wits, and critics. But the careless contempt of fame which mingled in him with so fierce a hunger for it kept it long a matter of doubt whether the immense reputation of these works belonged to him or not; and it would appear that his own personality, the size and rude splendor of his individual character, had at least as much to do with his position as the doubtful glory of an anonymous publication. The vicar of Laracor was not sufficiently important to be chosen as the representative of the Irish Church—but Jonathan Swift was; and though the bishops schemed against him in his absence when he seemed to have failed, no one seems to have ventured to suggest that he was too humble a person to hold that representative post. The book which dazzled English society and set all the wits talking was by no means the kind of book to support ecclesiastical dignity. It was indeed by way of being a vindication of the superiority of the Anglican Church over Rome on the one hand, and the dissenters on the other; but the tremendous raid against false pretenses, hypocrisy, and falsehood which is its real scope, was executed with such a riot and madness of laughter, and unscrupulous derision of everything that came in the satirist's way, as had scarcely been known in English speech before. The mockery was at once brilliant and careless, dashed about hither and thither in a sort of giant's play, full of the coarsest metaphors, the finest wit, indignation, ridicule, fun, almost too wild and reckless to be called cynical, though penetrated with the profoundest cynicism and disbelief of any good. The power which still lives and asserts itself in those strange and often detestable pages, must strike even the

SERVARE MODUM FINEMQUE TUERI NATURAMQUE SEQUI

Dominus Gulielmus Temple
Eques Baronettus Ser.^s et Pot.^s Regina Britanniæ Regis ad Ord.^s Fæd ─
Belgij Legatus Extr.^s et apud Tractatus pacis tam Aquisgrani quam ─
Neomagi Legatus Mediat.^r Eiusdem Ser.^s Regis 2 Secretioribus Consiliis.

SIR WILLIAM TEMPLE.

ENGRAVED BY R. A. MULLER, FROM AN ENGRAVING IN THE BRITISH MUSEUM,
AFTER A PAINTING BY SIR PETER LELY.

reader to whom they are most abhorrent. And the standard of taste was different in the reign of Anne, and critics were not easily alarmed. To some readers the most desperate satire that was ever written appeared a delightful piece of wit.

William Penn sent to the author from America a gammon of bacon on the score of having been "often greatly amused by thy *Tale*," and a hundred years later it "delighted beyond description" the robust mind of William Cobbett, so that he forgot that he had not supped and preferred the book to a bed. The effect upon the general mind of his contemporaries was equally great; and notwithstanding the immense difference of taste and public feeling it has never lost its place among English classics. Many indeed were horrified by its audacious treatment of the most sacred things, and the objection of Queen Anne to give its author a bishopric would probably have been shared by nine tenths of her subjects. The "Tale of a Tub" is one of those books which furnish a test of literary character. Like the man who was bound to hear the Ancient Mariner, and whom that mystic personage knew whenever he saw him, the reader of Swift's great work must be born with the faculty necessary for due appreciation and understanding. It is not a power communicable, any more than it is possible to explain the story of the albatross, and the curse that fell upon its slayer. The greater part of the public take both for granted, and remain in a respectful ignorance. To such Swift's work is little better than a dust-heap of genius, in which there are diamonds and precious things imbedded, which flash at every turning over; but the broken bits of treasure are mixed up with choking dust and dreary rubbish, as well as the offensive garbage which revolts the searcher. The dedication of the work to Prince Posterity is thus wholly justified, and at the same time a failure. It stands in the highest rank of classic satire, and yet to the mass of readers it is nothing but a name.

It is characteristic, however, of the man that he should have tossed into the world without a name a book which made a greater impression than any contemporary publication, enjoying no doubt the wonders and queries, yet scorning to make himself dependent upon so small a thing as a book for his reputation and influence.   He was no more disposed than the most sensitive of authors to let another man claim the credit of it, yet proud enough in native arrogance to hold himself independent of such aids to advancement, and thus to prove his scorn of the world's opinion, even when he sought its applauses most.   Whether this work had anything to do with his introduction to the society of the coffee-houses, and the wits of London, we are not told.   He was addressed by Addison as "the most Agreeable Companion, the Truest Friend, and the Greatest Genius of his age," very shortly after the publication of his great satire; so that it is probable he already enjoyed the advantage of its fame, without seeming to do so.   The friendship of Addison was a better thing than the admiration of the crowd, and notwithstanding Swift's imperious temper and arrogant ways, it is just to add that he always numbered among his friends the best and greatest of his time.

On a first accost, it would not seem that his manners were ingratiating.   This story, which is told of Swift's appearance at the St. James coffee-house is amusing, and may be true.

They had for several successive days observed a strange clergyman come into the house who seemed entirely unacquainted with any of those who frequented it, and whose custom was to lay down his hat on a table and walk backward and forward at a good pace, for half an hour or an hour, without speaking to any mortal, or seeming in the least to attend to anything that was going forward there.   He then used to take up his hat, pay his money at the bar, and walk away without opening his lips.   On one particular evening, as Mr. Addison and the rest were observing him, they saw him cast his eyes several times on a gentleman in boots who seemed to be just come out of the country, and at last advance, as if intending to address him. Eager to hear what this dumb, mad parson had to say, they all quitted their seats to get near him. Swift went up to the country gentleman, and in a very abrupt manner, without any previous salute, asked him, "Pray, sir, do you remember any good weather in the world?" The country gentleman, after staring a little at the peculiarity of his manner, answered, "Yes, sir, I remember a great deal of good weather in my time." "That is more," rejoined Swift, "than I can say. I never remember any weather that was not too hot or too cold, or too wet or too dry; but however God Almighty contrives at the end of the year it is all very well." With which remark he took up his hat, and without uttering a syllable more, or taking the least notice of any one, walked out of the coffee-house.

His whimsical humor, and love of making the spectators stare, remained a characteristic of Swift all his life.

These beginnings of social life were, however, past, and no one was better known or more warmly welcomed, when he appeared with his wig new curled, and his azure eyes aglow, than the Irish parson, waiting upon Providence and the Whigs, whose political pamphlets, and papers in the "Tatler," and malicious practical joking with poor Partridge, the astrologer, made him, at each appearance, a more notable figure to all the lookers-on. His eyes must have been on fire under those expressive brows when he came to London in 1710, resolved this time to be put off by Whig blandishments no longer, but to try what the other side would do. The other side received him with open arms, and the most instant appreciation of what he was worth to them and what he could do. Harley was not great in any sense of the word, but if he had shown as much insight in the conduct of public affairs as he did in his perception of the workmen best adapted to his purpose, in the struggle upon which he had entered, he would have been the most successful of ministers. He told Swift that his colleagues and himself had been afraid of none but him in the ranks of their enemies, and that they had resolved to have him. And in proof

that they were ready to do anything to secure his services, they
pushed on and decided as soon as might be his suit for the
church, which had hung in the balance so long, was as good
as granted, now as far off as ever.   It was settled at once, to
Swift's great triumph.   And to crown all, the new minister,
the greatest man in England, called him Jonathan!—of all
wonderful things, what could be more wonderful than that this
great wit, this powerful and pitiless satirist, this ambitious man,
should be altogether overcome with pleasure when Harley
called him by his Christian name!   Was it mere servility, vanity, the flattered weakness of a hanger-on in a great man's
familiarity, as everybody says?   It is hard to believe this,
though it is taken for granted on all sides.   Swift seems, at
all events, to have had a real affection for the shifty minister,
who received him in so different a fashion from that of his
former masters.   He flung himself into all the backstair intrigues, and collogued with Abigail Masham, and took his
share in every plot.   When Harley was stabbed, Swift felt
for him all the anxiety of a brother.   He threw himself into
the " Examiner," the new Tory organ, with fervor and enthusiasm, and expounded the principles of his party and set their
plans before the public with a force and clearness which nobody but he, his patrons declared, possessed.   The two statesmen, Harley and Bolingbroke, who were so little like each
other, so ill calculated to draw together, were alike in this:
that neither could be flattering enough or kind enough to the
great vassal whom they had secured.   He seems to have
thought of himself that he was a sort of third consul, an un-
official sharer of their power.

  This extraordinary episode in the life of a man of Swift's
profession, and so little likely to come to such promotion,
lasted three years; and the history of it is not less remarkable than the fact.   It was a period of the greatest intellec-

DELANY'S HOUSE AT DELVILLE, WHERE SWIFT STAYED.

DRAWN BY HARRY FENN. ENGRAVED BY C. A. POWELL.

tual activity and brilliancy in Swift's career, and besides his
hard political work in the "Examiner" and elsewhere, he
flung from him, amid the exhilarating appreciation of the
great world and his patrons, a number of the best of his
lighter productions. But nothing that he ever wrote can be
compared to the letters in which the story of this period is
told, since nowhere else do we find the charm of humanity,
which is more great and attractive even than genius. As if
the rule of paradox was to prevail in his life as well as in his
wit, this cynic, misanthrope, and satirist, ignoring love and
every softer thought, exhibits himself once to us in an abandon
and melting of the heart such as common men are as little
capable of as they are of his fierce laughter and bitter jests.
If it is the true man whom we see in these unpremeditated
and careless pages, written before he got up of a morning,
or in the evening when he came home from his entertain-
ments, with the chairmen still wrangling over their sixpences
outside, how different is that man from the other who storms
and laughs and mocks humanity, and sees through all its miserable pretenses without a thought of pardon or excuse! The
"Journal" letters addressed to the ladies in Dublin, Madam P.
P. T. and Madam Elderby, the two women who shared his
every thought, now so well known as the "Journal to Stella,"
are, of all Swift's works, the only productions that touch the
heart. They are not to be numbered among his "works" at
all: publication of any kind never seems to have occurred to
him, while writing: they are as frank as Pepy's, and far more
simple and true. They are English history and London life,
and the eighteenth century, with its mannerisms and quaint-
ness, all in one; and beyond and above every circumstance,
they are Swift as he was in his deepest soul,— not as he
appeared to men,— a human being full of tenderness, full of
fun and innocent humor, full of genius and individual nature,

but, above all, of true affection, the warmest domestic love. Passion is not in those delightful pages; but the endearing playfulness, the absolute freedom of self-revelation, the tender intimacy and confidence of members of the same family, whose interests and subjects of thought and talk and merry jests and delusions are one. They describe every day — nay, hour — of his life, every little expedition, all the ups and downs of his occupations and progress, with the boundless freedom and sportive extravagance, the unimpassioned, unabashed adoration of something warmer than a father, more indulgent, more admiring than a brother, yet brother, father, lover, and friend all in one.

Only to a woman could such letters have been addressed, and few women reading them will be disposed to pity Stella or think her life one of blight or injury. Without these the life of the dean would not have touched our human sympathies at all, but now that time has let us thus fully into his confidence, and opened to our sight what was never intended for any but hers and those of her shadow, her guardian, the humble third in this profound and perfect union, it is with moistened eyes that we read the ever living record. There is nothing in the coarse and struggling potency of those books which critics applaud, that comes within a hundred miles of the delightful life and ease of these outpourings of Swift's innermost soul. The "Tale of a Tub," the "Battle of the Books," retain a sort of galvanic existence, but are for the greater part insupportable to the honest readers who have no tradition of superior acumen and perception to maintain. But when we turn to the "Journal," the clean and wholesome pages smile with a cordial life and reality. If there is here and there a phrase too broad for modern ears, it is nothing more than the language of the time, and has not a ghost of evil meaning in it. The big arrogant wit—not unused to bluster and brag, to act like a tyrant and speak like a bully

—meets us there defenseless, with the tenderest light upon his face, in his nightcap and without his wig, smiling over little M. D.'s letter in the wintry mornings, snatching a moment at bedtime when he is already "seepy," and can do nothing but bid "nite deelest dea M. D. nite deelest loques," making his mouth, he says, as if he were saying the broken, childish words, retiring into the sanctuary of the little language with an infinite sense of consolation and repose. Outside it may be he swaggered and defed all men, even his patrons; but here an exquisite softness comes over him. However he may be judged or mistaken in the world, he is always understood by the women in that secret world where they make their comments on whatever happens, and merrily answer back again with their criticisms, their strictures, no more afraid of that impetuous, angry genius than if he had been the meekest of rural priests. It is this that has got Swift his hold upon many a reader, who, beginning by hating him, the coarse and bitter wit, the scorner of men and crusher of women's hearts, has suddenly found his own heart melt in his breast to see the giant lay by his thunders and·prattle like an old gossip, like a tender mother, father, all in one, in the baby-talk that first had opened to him the knowledge of all that is sweetest in life. We do not understand the man, much less the woman, who can read without forgiving to Swift all his brutalities, as indeed most women who encountered him seem to have done without that argument. He would treat the fine ladies with the most imperious rudeness, giving forth his rule that it was they who should make advances to him, not he to them, yet captivating even those who resisted in the end.

The little language which this fierce satirist and cynic dared to put in writing, the only man ever so bold as to pay such homage to affection, puzzled beyond measure his first editors and expositors, who, with a horrified prudery, seem to have done their best to interpret and restore it to decorum and dignity ; but it has now become the point in his story which is most tenderly recollected, his sacred reconciliation with mankind. A homeless boy, with none of the traditions of a family, finding his unlovely life not less but more unpromising in his first experiences of Temple's luxurious English home, what a sudden fountain of sweetness must have opened to him in the prattle of the delightful child, which was a new revelation to his heart—revelation of all that kindred meant, and delightful intimacy and familiar love. His little star of life never waned to Swift: Stella grew old, but never outgrew the little language, and every young woman had something in her of the sprightly creature that loved to do his bidding, the P. P. T. who held her own, and put him upon his best behavior often, yet never was other than the "deelest little loque" whom he bantered and laughed at with soft tears of tenderness in his eyes. "Better, thank God, and M. D.'s prayers," he says among the private scribbles of his daily diary, which neither she nor any one was ever meant to see. Nevertheless, even while he was writing this "Journal," which is the record of a tender intimacy so remarkable, Swift was meddling with the education of another girl, incautiously, foolishly, who was not of the uninflammable nature of Stella, but a hot-headed, passionate creature who did not at all imagine that the mere

> . . . delight he took
> To see the virgin mind her book

was all Dr. Swift meant by his talk and attention. Swift says nothing of this pupil in the "Journal." He mentions his dinners at Mrs. Vanhomrigh's, and her handsome daughter, but he does not tell Madam P. P. T. that he had given one of his usual caressing names to this girl, whose early beauty and frank devotion had pleased him. There is, indeed, no shadow

MARLEY ABBEY, THE RESIDENCE OF VANESSA,
NOW CALLED SELBRIDGE ABBEY.

DRAWN BY HARRY FENN. ENGRAVED BY R. C. COLLINS.

of Vanessa anywhere visible, though the brief mention of her name shows that the second story, which was to be so fatally and painfully mingled with the first, had already begun.

The three years of Swift's stay in England were the climax of his life. They raised him higher than ever a simple parson had been raised before, and made of him (or so, at least, he believed) a power in the state. It has been doubted whether he was really so highly trusted, so much built upon, as he thought. The great lords who delighted in Swift's talk, and called him Jonathan, did not, perhaps, follow his advice and accept his guidance, as he supposed. He says, jestingly — yet half, perhaps, with an uneasy meaning,—that everything that was said between himself and Harley as they traveled sociably in my Lord Treasurer's coach to Windsor, might have been told at Charing Cross; but this was a rare admission, and generally he was very full of the schemes of the ministers and their consultations, and his own important share in them. He seems to have constituted himself the patron of everybody he knew, really providing for a considerable number, and largely undertaking for others, though it was long before he got anything for himself. The following anecdote gives an unpleasant view from outside of his demeanor and habits. It is from Bishop Kennett's diary during the year 1713, the last of Swift's importance:

Swift came into the coffee-room, and had a bow from everybody save me. When I came to the antechamber to wait before prayers, Dr. Swift was the principal man of talk and business, and acted as minister of requests. He was soliciting the Earl of Arran to speak to his brother the Duke of Ormond to get a chaplain's place established in the garrison of Hull for Mr. Fiddes, a clergyman in that neighborhood, who had lately been in jail and published sermons to pay fees. He was promising Mr. Thorold to undertake with my Lord Treasurer that according to his position he should obtain a salary of £200 per annum as minister of the English Church in Rotterdam. He stopped F. Gwynne, Esq.,

8

going in with the red bag to the Queen, and told him aloud he had something to say to him from my Lord Treasurer. He talked with the son of Dr. Davenant, to be sent abroad, and took out his pocket-book, and wrote down several things as *memoranda* to do for him. He turned to the fire, and took out his gold watch, and, telling them the time of day, complained it was very late. A gentleman said, "It goes too fast." "How can I help it," says the Doctor, "if the courtiers give me a watch that won't go right?" Then he instructed a young nobleman that the best poet in England was Mr. Pope (a papist), who had begun a translation of Homer into English verse, for which, he said, he must have them all subscribe. "For," says he, "the author shall not begin to print it till I have a thousand guineas for him." Lord Treasurer, after leaving the Queen, came through the room, beckoning Dr. Swift to follow him; both went off just before prayers.

But the account of the patronage which he exercised, and the brag and general "swagger" of his demeanor, though it is by no means invisible in the "Journal," has a different aspect there, where he tells all about his favor and power, to please his correspondents, with a good excuse in this tender reason for magnifying all that happens to him. It was, indeed, a position to turn even the soundest head, and Swift had thirsted all his life for power, for notability, for that buoyant sense of being on the top of the wave which was so contrary to all his previous experience. His own satirical account of himself, as desiring literary eminence only to make up for the mistake of not being born a lord, is a self-contemptuous way of stating the thirst he had to be foremost, to be doing, to be capable of moving the world. And he may very well be excused for thinking now that he had done so.

Amid the many disappointments of his life he had these three years of triumph, which are much for a man to have. If there was a certain vulgarity in his enjoyment of them, there was at the same time a great deal of active kindness, and though he might brag of the services he did, he yet did service and remembered his friends, and helped as he could those hangers-on and waiters upon Providence who, in those days, were always about a minister's antechamber. It is unnecessary to attempt to go over again the story of the politics of the time, in which he was so powerful an agent. To see Swift moving about in his gown and wig, with his eyes, "azure as the heavens," glowing keen from underneath his deep brows, sometimes full of sport and laughter and tender kindness, sometimes with something "awful" in their look, sometimes dazzling with humorous tyranny and command, is more interesting than to fathom over again for the hundredth time the confusing intrigues of the age. One thing is evident, that while he served others he got nothing for himself: the bishopric so long longed for did not come, nor even a fat English deanery, which would have been worth the having and kept him near the center of affairs. Was Harley too, disposed to flatter rather than promote his Jonathan? or was it the queen's determined prejudice, and conviction that the "Tale of a Tub" was no fit foundation for a miter? The latter would have been little wonderful, for Swift had taken pains to embroil himself with the court, by a coarse and ineffective satire called the "Windsor Prophecy," which no doubt amused the hostile coteries, yet could not but do the rash writer harm.

At last, just before the fall of Harley, preferment was found for the champion who had served him so well. It was the last that Swift would have chosen for himself—a kind of dignified banishment and exile from all he loved best. There was a question between the deanery of St. Patrick's and that of Windsor, he himself says. Had he gone to the royal borough, what a curious change might have come to all his after life! Would Stella, one wonders, have found a red-roofed house under the cloister walls? and the dean lived, perhaps, to get the confidence of Queen Caroline, a queen worth pleasing? and looked upon the world with azure eyes softened by prosperity

from the storied slopes, and worn his ribbon of the Garter with
a proud inflation of the bosom which had always sighed for
greatness?   How many differences, how much softening, ex-
panding, almost elevation, might not the kind hand of Fortune
work in such great but troubled natures were it allowed to
smooth and caress the roughness away!

When the issue of the conflict between Harley and Bolingbroke became too evident to be doubted, Swift showed the
softer side of his character in a very unexpected way.   He ran
away from the catastrophe like a nervous woman, hiding himself in a country parsonage till the blow should be struck and
the calamity be overpast, a very curious piece of moral timidity
or nervous over-sensitiveness, for which we are entirely unpre-
pared.   It was less extraordinary that he should write to offer
himself to Harley as a companion in his solitude when the minister was fairly ousted, although even then Bolingbroke was
bidding eagerly for his services.   But whether Swift would
have accepted these offers, or would have carried his evidently
genuine attachment to Harley so far as permanently to withdraw with him from public life, was never known.   For the victory of St. John was short indeed.   "The Earl of Oxford was
removed on Tuesday, the Queen died on Sunday.   What a
world is this, and how does Fortune banter us!" writes Bolingbroke.   It was such a stroke of the irony of fate as Swift himself might have invented, and St. John applauded with the
laughter of the philosopher.   There was an end of political
power for both, and the triumph and greatness of Swift's
reflected glory was over without hope of renewal.

He had now nothing to do but to return to Ireland, so long
neglected, the country of his disappointments, which did not
love him, and which he did not love, where his big genius (he
thought) had not room enough to breathe, where society was
small and provincial, and life flat and bare, and only a few

familiar friends appreciated him or knew what he was. How he was to make himself the idol of that country, a kind of king in it, and gain power of a different kind from any he had yet wielded, was as yet a secret hidden in the mists of the future to Swift and everybody around. His account of himself when he got home to his dull deanery, "a vast unfurnished house," with a few servants in it, "all on board wages," is melancholy enough. "I live a country life in town, see nobody, and go every day once to prayers, and hope in a few months to grow as stupid as the present situation of affairs will require," but he consoles himself: "after all, parsons are not such bad company, especially when they are *under subjection; and I let none but such come near me*," a curious statement, in which the great satirist, as often before, gives a stroke of his idle sword at himself.

But Swift was not long left in this stagnation. Extreme quiet is in many cases but a cover for brewing mischief, and the dean had not long returned to Ireland when that handsome daughter of Mrs. Vanhomrigh, of whom he had said so little in his letters, found herself, on her mother's death, drawn to Ireland, and the neighborhood of her tutor and correspondent. It is curious to find so many links to Ireland in this little company. Stella had a farm in Meath left to her by Sir William Temple, Vanessa, "a small property at Celbridge," to which it suited her to retire. And thus there were gathered together within a short distance the dean himself in his dull house, the assured and quiet possessor of his tenderest affections in Dublin near him, and the impassioned girl who had declared for him love of a very different kind, at Marley Abbey, within the reach of a ride. That Swift had a heart large enough to admit on his own terms many women is very evident, and that he had a fondness for Vanessa among the rest; but how far he was to blame for her fatal passion, it is scarcely possible to decide.

The story of their connection, as told from his side of the question in the poem of " Cadenus and Vanessa," shows an uncon-
sciousness and innocence of purpose which takes all the responsibility of her infatuation from the dean, and shows him in a light
all too artless.

> The innocent delight he took,
> To see the virgin mind her book,
> Was but the master's secret joy
> In school to hear the finest boy.

But this was not the light in which the headstrong young
woman, who made no secret of her love, and filled him with
"shame, disappointment, guilt, remorse," by the revelation, regarded his attentions. Their correspondence went on for
nearly ten years. It is a painful correspondence, as the out-
pouring of a woman's passion for a man who does not respond
to it must always be; but Swift never seems to have fostered
that passion, nor to have done anything but discourage and
subdue a love so embarrassing and troublesome.

And now comes in the mystery which everybody has discussed, but which none have brought to any certain conclusion.
In 1716, two years after Swift's return to Ireland, it is said that
he married Stella, thus putting himself at once out of all possibility of marrying Miss Vanhomrigh (which might have been a
motive) and satisfying Stella, as the notion goes. Scott re-
ceives the statement as proved; so does Mr. Craik, Swift's last,
and a most conscientious and careful biographer. The evidence for it is that Lord Orrery and Dr. Delany, the earliest
writers on the subject, both assert it ("if my informations are
right," as the former says) as a supposition universally believed
in society; and that the fact was told by the Bishop of Clogher,
who performed the ceremony, to Bishop Berkeley, who told it
to his wife, who told it after her husband's death, and long after
the event, to George Monck Berkeley, who tells the story.

But Bishop Berkeley was in Italy at the time and could not have been told, though he might have heard it at second-hand from his pupil, the Bishop of Clogher's son. We wonder if an inheritance or the legitimacy of a child would be considered proved by such evidence, or whether the prevailing sense of society that such a thing ought to have taken place has not a large share in the common belief. At all times, as at the present moment, wherever a close friendship between man and woman exists (and the very fact of such rumors makes it extremely rare), suggestions of the same description float in the air. Nobody supposes, if the marriage took place at all, that it was anything more than a mere form. It was performed, if performed at all, in the garden without any formal or legal preliminaries. Supposing such a fictitious rite to have any justification in Irish law, we wonder what the authorities of the church would have had to say to two high dignitaries who united to perform an act so disorderly and contrary to ecclesiastical decorum, if to nothing else. It is totally unlike Swift, whose feeling for the church was strong, to have used her ordinances so disrespectfully, and most unlike all we know of Stella that she should have consented to so utterly false a relationship. However, the question is one which the reader will decide according to his own judgment, and upon which no one can speak with authority. Mr. Forster, of all Swift's biographers the most elaborate and anxious, did not get so far in his work as to examine the evidence, yet intimates his disbelief of the story. We do not need, however, to have recourse to the expedient of a marriage to explain how the story of Vanessa might have been a pain and offense to Stella. Swift had not in this particular been frank with his friends, and the discovery, so near them, of a woman making so passionate a claim upon his affections must have conveyed the shock at once of a deception and an unpardonable intrusion to one who was proudly con-

scious of being his most trusted confidant and closest companion.   Whatever were the rights of the case, however, nobody can now know.   Whether Vanessa had heard the rumor
of the private marriage, whether she conceived that a desperate appeal to his dearest friend might help her own claim,
or whether mere suspicion and misery, boiling over, found expression in the hasty letter to Stella which she wrote at the
crisis of her career, is equally unessential.   She did write, and
Stella, surprised and offended, showed the letter to Swift.
Nothing can be more tragic than the events that follow.
Swift, in one of those wild bursts of passion which were beyond the control of reason, rode out at once to the unfortunate young woman's house.   He burst in without a word,
threw her own letter on the table before her, and rode off
again like a whirlwind.   Vanessa came of a short-lived race,
and was then, at thirty-four, the last of her family.   She never
recovered the blow, but, dying soon after, directed her letters
and the poem which contained the story of her love and his
coldness to be published.   This was not done for nearly a
century; and now more than half of another has gone, but
the story is as full of passion and misery, as unexplained, as
ever.   This was one of the occupations of Swift's stagnant
time.   He fled, as he had done at the moment of Harley's
fall, that, at least, he might not see what was going to happen.

But a little while longer was the other, the love of his life,
spared to him.   Five years after the tragical end of Vanessa,
Stella too died, after long suffering.   There is a second story,
of equally doubtful authenticity and confused and extraordinary
details, about a proposed tardy acknowledgment of the apoc-
ryphal marriage; but whether it was he or she who suggested this, whether it was he or she who found it "too
late," whether there was any reality in it at all, no one
has ever determined.   Stella's illness grew serious while Swift

GEORGE, EARL OF BERKELEY.

FROM AN UNFINISHED ENGRAVING, IN THE BRITISH MUSEUM,
ATTRIBUTED TO DAVID LOGGAN.

was absent, and his anguish at the news was curiously mingled
with an overwhelming dread lest she should die at the deanery,
and thus compromise her reputation and his own; perhaps,
too, lest the house to which he must return should be made intolerable to him by the shadow of such an event. That he
should have kept away, with his usual terror of everything
painful, was entirely in keeping with his character. But the
first alarm passed away, and Swift was in the deanery when
this great sorrow overtook him. He who had kept a letter for
an hour without daring to open it, in which he trembled to find
the news of her death, now shut himself up heartbroken in his
solitary house, and, somewhat calmed by the irrevocable,— as
grief, however desperate, always must be,— proceeded to give
himself what consolation was possible by writing a "Character,"
as was the fashion of the time, of "the truest, most virtuous,
and valuable friend I, or perhaps any other person, was ever
blessed with." The calm after the storm, but a calm of sober
despair and dread, unreal composure, is in this strange document. He wrote till "my head aches, and I can write no
more," and on the third day resumed and completed the
strange and melancholy narrative.

This is the night of her funeral, which my sickness will not suffer me
to attend. It is now nine at night, and I am removed into another
apartment, that I may not see the light in the Church, which is just over
against the window of my bedchamber.

She was buried in his own cathedral by torchlight, as the
custom was; but he would no more bear the glimpses of that
awful light through the window, than he could witness the putting away of all that remained of Stella in the double gloom of
the vault and the night. In that other apartment he concluded
his sad panegyric, the story of all she was and did, showing
with intense but subdued eloquence that there was no fault in

her. "There is none like her, none." This is the burden of
the old man's self-restrained anguish, the tragedy of his age,
as it is the young lover's pæan of triumph. The truest, most
valuable friend that ever man had — and now her beautiful life
was ended, to be his consolation no more. He had a lock of
her hair in his possession somewhere, either given him then or
at some brighter moment, which was found after his death, as
all the world knows, with these words written upon the paper
that contained it: "Only a woman's hair." Only all the softness, the brightness, the love and blessing of a life; only all
that the heart had to rest upon of human solace; only that —
no more. He who had thanked God and M. D.'s prayers for
his better health, had now no one to pray for him, or to receive his confidences. It was over, all that best of life — as
if it had never been.

It is easy to expand such a text, and many have done it.
In the mean time, before these terrible events had occurred,
while Vanessa's letters were still disturbing his peace, and death
had as yet touched none of his surroundings, he had accomplished the greatest literary work of his life, that by which
every child knows Swift's name — the travels of the famous
Gulliver. The children have made their selection with an un-
erring judgment which is above criticism, and have taken Lilliput and Brobdingnag into their hearts, rejecting all the rest.
That Swift had a meaning, bitter and sharp, even in the most
innocent part of that immortal fable, and meant to strike a blow
at politicians and generals, and the human race, with its puny
wars, and glories, and endless vanities and foolishness, is evident enough; and it was for this that the people of his time
seized upon the book with breathless interest, and old Duchess
Sarah in her old age chuckled and forgave the dean. But the
vast majority of his readers have not so much as known that
he meant anything except the most amusing and witty fancy,

the keenest comic delineation of impossible circumstances.
That delightful Irish bishop, if ever he was, who declared that
"the book was full of improbable lies, and for his part he
hardly believed a word of it," is the only critic we want. "'Gulliver's Travels' is almost the most delightful children's book
ever written," says Mr. Leslie Stephen, no small authority. It
had no doubt been talked over and read to the ladies, who, it
would incidentally appear, had not liked the "Tale of a Tub."
But Swift was at home when he wrote "Gulliver," and had no
need of a journal to communicate his proceedings.

Between 1714 and 1726, for a dozen years, he remained in
Ireland without intermission, altogether apart from public life.
At the latter date he went to London, probably needing, after
the shock of Miss Vanhomrigh's death, and the grievous sense
he must have had that it was he who had killed her, a change
of scene; and it was then that "Gulliver" was published. The
latter portions of it which the children have rejected we are glad
to have no space to dwell upon. The bitterness, passion, and
misery of them are beyond parallel. One would like to have
any ground for believing that the Houyhnhms and the rest
came into being after Stella's death; but this was not the case.
She was only a woman, and was not, after all, of such vital
importance in the man's existence. Withdrawal from the life
he loved, confinement in a narrow sphere, the disappointment
of a soul which felt itself born for greatness, and had tasted the
high excitements of power, but now had nothing to do but
fight over the choir with his archbishop, and give occasion for
a hundred anecdotes in the Dublin coteries, had matured the
angry passion in him and soured the sweetness of nature. Few
people now when they take up their "Gulliver" go beyond
Brobdingnag. The rest is like a succession of bad dreams, the
confused miseries of a fever. To think that in a deanery, that
calm seat of ecclesiastical luxury, within sound of the cathedral

bells and the choristers' chants, a brain so dark and distracted, and dreams so terrible, should have found shelter! They are all the more bitter and appalling from their contrast with the surroundings among which they had their disastrous birth.

The later part of Swift's life, however, had occupation of a very different and nobler kind. The Ireland he knew was so different from the Ireland with which we are acquainted, that to contemplate the two is apt to give a sort of moral vertigo, a giddiness of the intellect, to the observer. Swift's Ireland was the country of the English-Irish, ultra-Protestant, like the real Ireland only in the keenness of its politics and the sharpness of its opposition to imperial measures. It was Ireland with a parliament of her own, and many of the privileges which are now her highest aspirations, yet she was not content. Swift, in speaking of the people, the true Irish, the Catholic masses, who at that moment bore their misery with a patience inconceivable, said of them that they were no more considerable than the women and children, a race so utterly trodden down and subdued that there was no need for the politician to take them into account. The position of the predominant class was almost like that of white men among the natives of a savage country, or at least like that of the English in India, the confident and assured rulers of a subject race. Nevertheless, these men were full of a sort of national feeling, and ready to rise up in hot and not ineffectual opposition when need was, and reckon themselves Irish, whereas no sahib has ever reckoned himself Indian. The real people of Ireland were held under the severest yoke, but those gentlemen who represented the nation can scarcely be said to have been oppressed. Their complaint was that Englishmen were put into vacant posts, that their wishes were disregarded, and their affairs neglected, complaints which even prosperous Scotland has been known to make. They were affected, however, as well as the race which

ST. PATRICK'S CATHEDRAL, DUBLIN.

DRAWN BY HARRY FENN. ENGRAVED BY C. A. POWELL.

they kept under their feet, by the intolerable law which suppressed woolen manufactures in Ireland, and it was on this subject that Swift first broke silence, and appeared as the national champion, recommending to his countrymen such reprisals as the small can employ against the great, in the form of a proposal that Irishmen should use Irish manufactures only, a proposal by no means unlikely to be carried out should an Irish parliament ever exist again.

The commotion produced by this real and terrible oppression was nothing, however, to that called forth by an innocent attempt to give a copper coinage—the most convenient of circulating mediums—to Ireland. Nothing could have been more harmless, more useful and necessary in reality, and there is no reason to suppose that dishonesty of any kind was involved. But the public mind was embittered by the fact that the patent had been granted to one of King George's German favorites, and by her sold to Wood, an Englishman, who was supposed to be about to make an enormous profit out of the country by half-pence not worth their nominal value. Such an idea stirred the prejudices and fears of the very lowest, and would even now rouse the ignorant into rage and panic. Whether Swift shared that natural and national, if unreasonable, outburst of indignation and alarm to the full extent, or if he threw himself into it with the instinct of an agitator foreseeing the capabilities of the subject, it is difficult to tell. But the "Drapier's Letters" gave to the public outcry so powerful a force of resistance, and excited the entire country into such unanimity and opposition, that the English Government was forced to withdraw from this attempt, and the position of the Irish nation, as an oppressed yet not unpowerful entity, still able to face its tyrants and protest against their careless sway, became distinctly apparent. It is strange that a man who hated Ireland, and considered himself

an exile in her, should have been the one to claim for her
an independence, a freedom she had never yet possessed, and
should have been able to inspire at once the subject and the
ruling race with the sense that they had found a champion capable of all things, and through whom for the first time their
voice might be heard in the world. The immediate result was to
Swift a popularity beyond bounds. The people he despised
were seized with an adoration for him which was shared by
the class to which he himself belonged—perhaps the first subject on which they had agreed.   "When he returned from
England in 1726 bells were rung, bonfires lighted, and a guard
of honor escorted him to the deanery.   Towns voted him their
freedom and received him as a prince.   When Walpole spoke
of arresting him a prudent friend told the minister that the
messenger would require a guard of 10,000 soldiers."   When
the crowd which had gathered to see an eclipse disturbed him
by the hum they made, Swift sent out to tell them that the
event was put off by order of the dean, and the simple-minded
people dispersed obediently! Had he been so minded, and had
he fully understood and loved the race over which his great
and troubled spirit had gained such power, much might perhaps have been ameliorated in that unfortunate country, so
cursed in her friends as in her foes, and much in the soul con-
suming itself in angry inactivity with no fit work in hand.   But
it would have taken a miracle indeed to have turned this Englishman born in Ireland, this political churchman and hater
of papists and dissenters, into the savior of the subject race.
That he was, however, deeply struck with an impression of
their misery, and that his soul, always so ready to break forth
upon the cruelty, the falsehood, the barbarous misconception
of men by men, found in their wrongs a subject upon which he
could scarcely exaggerate, is apparent enough.   His " Modest
Proposal for Preventing the Children of the Poor in Ireland

from Being a Burden to their Parents or Country" is one of those pieces of terrible satire which lacerate the heart. Tears as of blood are in it, a passion of indignant pity, and fury, and despair. " Eat them, then, since there 's nothing else to be done with them," he says, detailing with elaborate composure the way to do it and the desirableness of such a supply of delicate food. The reader, unwarned and simple-minded, might almost, with a gasp of horror, take the proposal for genuine. But Swift's meaning was really more terrible than cannibalism. It was the sense that these children, the noblest fruit of nature, were in truth the embarrassment, the fatal glut of a miserable race, that forced this dreadful irony upon him. And what picture could be more terrible than that of the childless old man with his bleeding heart, himself deserted of all that made life sweet, thus facing the world with scorn so infinite that it transcends all symbols of passion, bidding it consume what it has brought forth ?

But Swift, unfortunately for himself and her, loved Ireland as little when he thus made himself her champion as he had done throughout his life. At all times his longing eyes were turned toward the country in which life was, and power, and friends, and fame. Though he was aware he was growing old and ought to be "done with this world," he yet cries aloud his desire "to get into a better before I was called into the best, and not die here in a rage like a poisoned rat in a hole,"—a terrific image, and one of those phrases that burn and glow with a pale light of despair. But he never got into that better world he longed for. The slow years crept over him, and he lived on, making existence tolerable by such expedients as he could, a wonderful proof how the body will resist all the frettings of the soul, yet growing more angry, more desperate, more subject to the bitter passions which had broken forth even in his best days, as he grew older and had fewer reasons for restraining himself. At last the great dean, the greatest genius of his age, the man of war and battle, of quip and jest, he who had thirsted to be doing through all his life, fell into imbecility and stupor, with occasional wild awakenings into consciousness which were still more terrible. He died, denuded of all things, in 1745, having lived till seventy-eight in spite of himself.

Ubi saeva indignatio
Cor ulterius lacerare nequit

is written on his tomb. No more can fiery wrath and indignation reach him where he lies by Stella's side in the aisle over against his chamber window. The touch of her quiet dust must have soothed, one would think, the last fever that lingered still in him even after death had done its worst.

Chapter IV

THE AUTHOR OF "ROBINSON CRUSOE"

THE age of Queen Anne was one which abounded in paradoxes, and loved them. It was an age when England was full of patriotic policy, yet every statesman was a traitor; when tradition was dear, yet revolution practicable; when speech was gross and manners unrefined, yet the laws of literary composition rigid, and correctness the test of poetry. It was full of high ecclesiasticism and strict Puritanism, sometimes united in one person. In it ignorance was most profound, yet learning most considered and prominent. An age when Parson Trulliber was not an unfit representative of the rural clergy, yet the public could be interested in such a recondite pleasantry as the " Battle of the Books," seems the strangest self-contradiction; yet so it was in this paradoxical age. No man lived who was a more complete paradox than Defoe. His fame is world-wide, yet all that is known of him is one or two of his least productions, and his busy life is ignored in the permanent place in literary history which he has secured. His characteristics as apart from his conduct, are all those of an honest man, but when that most important part of him is taken into the question it is difficult to pronounce him anything but a knave. His distinguishing literary quality is a minute truthfulness to fact which makes it almost impossible not to take what he says for gospel. But his constant inspiration is fiction, not to say, in some circumstances, falsehood. He spent his life in the highest endeavors that a man can engage in : in the work of persuading and influencing his country, chiefly for her good ; and he is remembered by a boy's book, which is indeed the first of boy's books, yet not much more. Through these contradictions we must push our way before we can reach to any clear idea of Defoe, the London tradesman who by times composed almost all the newspapers in London, wrote all the pamphlets, had his finger in every pie, and a share in all that was done, yet brought nothing out of it but a damaged reputation and an unhonored end.

It is curious that something of a similar fate should have happened to the other and greater figure, his contemporary, his enemy, in some respects his fellow-laborer, another and more brilliant slave of the government, which in itself had so little that was brilliant,— the great dean whose name has already appeared so often in these sketches. Swift, too, of all his books, is remembered chiefly by the book of the travels of "Gulliver," which, though full of a satirical purpose unknown to Defoe, has come to rank along with "Robinson Crusoe." We may say indeed that these two books form a class by themselves, of perennial enchantment for the young, and full of a curious and enthralling illusion which even in age we rarely shake off. Swift rises into bitter and terrible tragedy, while Defoe sinks into matter of fact and commonplace ; but the shipwrecked sailor on his desolate island, and the exile at the courts of Lilliput and Brobdingnag, both in the beginnings of their careers hold our imaginations captive, and are as fresh and as powerful to-day as when, the one in keen satire, the other in the legitimate way of business, they first made their appearance in the world. It is a singular link between the men who both did Harley's dirty work for him, and were subject to a leader so much smaller than themselves.

Daniel Defoe was born in London in 1661, of what would

seem to have been a respectable burgher family, only one
generation out of the country, which probably was why his
father, with yeomen and grazier relations in Northampton-
shire, was a butcher in town. The butcher's name, however, was
Foe; and whether the Defoe of his son was a mere pleasantry
upon his signature of D. Foe, or whether it embodied an intention of setting up for something better than the tradesman's
monosyllable, is a quite futile question upon which nobody can
throw any light. The boy was well educated, according to the
capabilities of his kindred, in a school at Newington, probably
intended for the sons of comfortable dissenting tradesmen, who
were to be devoted to the ministry, with the assistance in some
cases of a fund raised for that purpose. The master was good,
and if Defoe attained there even the rudiments of the information he afterward showed, and laid claim to, the education must
have been excellent indeed He claims to have known Latin,
Spanish, Italian, French, "and could read the Greek,"—which
latter is as much as could have been expected had he been
the most advanced of scholars,— besides an acquaintance with
science, geography, and history not to be surpassed, apparently, by any man of his time. "If I am a blockhead," he
says, "it was nobody's fault but my own," his father having
"spared nothing" on his education. Much of this information,
however, was no doubt picked up in the travels and much knock-
ing about of his early years, of which there is little record. He
would seem to have changed his mind about becoming a dissenting minister at an early age, and was probably a youth of
somewhat wandering tendencies, as he claims to have been
"out" with Monmouth, and does not appear in any recognized
occupation till after that unfortunate attempt. He must have
been twenty-four when he first becomes visible as a hosier in
Cornhill, which seems a very natural and indeed rather superior
beginning in life for the son of the butcher in Cripplegate.

He laid claim afterward to having been a trader,— not a shopkeeper,— a claim supported more or less from a source not
favorable to Defoe, by Oldmixon, who says that his only connection with the trade was that of "peddling to Portugal,"
whatever that may mean. We may take it for granted that he
had occasions of visiting the Continent in connection, one way
or other, with his trade. The volume of advice to shopkeepers
which is entitled the "Complete English Tradesman," written
and published in the latter part of his life, though it does not seem
to be taken by his biographers in general as any certain indica-
tion that he himself made his beginning in a shop, is nevertheless full of curious details of the life of the London shopkeeper
of his time, to which class he assuredly belonged. We learn
from this curious production that vanity was even more foolish
in the eighteenth century than it is now. We are acquainted
with sporting shopkeepers who ride to hounds, and with foolish
young men who fondly hope to be mistaken for "swells"; but
a shopkeeper in a wig and a sword passes the power of imagination. It is a droll example of the fallacy of all our fond retro-
spections and preference of the good old times to find that in
Defoe's day this was by no means an extraordinary circumstance. "The playhouses and balls," he says, "are more filled
with citizens and young tradesmen than with gentlemen and
families of distinction; the shopkeepers wear different garbs
than what they were wont to do, are decked out with long
wigs and swords, and all the frugal badges of trade are quite
disdained and cast aside."

We may take from this book as an illustration of the habits
of the age the following description of a young firm which is
clearly on the way to ruin:

They say there are two partners of them, but there had as good
be none, for they are never at home or in the shop. One wears a long
peruke and a sword, I hear, and you see him often at the ball and at

court, but very seldom in his shop, or waiting on his customers; and
the other, they say, lies abed till eleven o'clock every day, just comes
into the shop and shows himself, then stalks about to the tavern to take
a whet, then to the coffee-house to hear the news, comes home to dinner at one, takes a long sleep in his chair after it, and about four o'clock
comes into the shop for half an hour or thereabouts, then to the tavern,
where he stays till two in the morning, gets drunk, and is led home by
the watch, and so lies till eleven again; and thus he walks round like the
hand of a dial. And what will it all come to? They 'll certainly break.
They can't hold long.

The account of the shop kept by these two idle masters is
equally characteristic.

There is a good stock of goods in it, but there is nobody to serve
but a prentice boy or two and an idle journeyman. One finds them all
at play together rather than looking out for customers; and when you
come to buy, they look as if they did not care whether they showed you
anything or no. Then it is a shop always exposed; it is perfectly
haunted with thieves and shoplifters. They are nobody but raw boys
in it that mind nothing, so that there are more outcries of stop thief! at
their door, and more constables fetched to that shop than to all the shops
in the street.

The households of the soberer and more sensible members
of the craft are also open to grave animadversion. The ladies
are too fine; they treat their friends with wine or punch or
fine ale, and have their parlors set off with the tea-table and
the chocolate-pot, and the silver coffee-pot, and oftentimes an
ostentation of plate into the bargain, and they keep " three or
four maid servants, nay, sometimes five," and some a footman
besides, " for 't is an ordinary thing to see the tradesmen and
shopkeepers of London keep footmen, as well as the gentlemen.
Witness the infinite number of blue liveries which are so common now that they are called the tradesmens' liveries, and few
gentlemen care to give blue to their servants for that very
reason." Of the maids themselves, who ask " six, seven, nay

9*

eight pounds per annum" for their services, a terrible account
is given in a pamphlet published about 1725, where there is a
humorous description in the first person of a young woman who
comes to apply for the place of housemaid, evidently maid of all
work to the speaker, who lives with his sister, with a man and
maid for their household. She is so fine that Defoe himself
shows her into the parlor and keeps her company till his sister is ready, thinking her a gentlewoman come to pay a visit.
Perhaps it is not Defoe, but, with his usual skill, he makes
us think so. All these details bring before us the London of
his time. The mercers had their shops in Paternoster Row,
"where the spacious shops, back warehouses, skylights, and
other conveniences, made on purpose for their trade, are still
to be seen," where "they all grew rich and very seldom any
failed or miscarried," and also in Cornhill, where Defoe's own
establishment was, though there, apparently, business was carried on wholesale. It appears to him that trade is going
downhill fast when this order is changed, when Paul's Church-
yard is filled with cane-chair makers, and Cornhill with the
meanest of trades, even Cheapside itself, "how is it now filled
up with shoemakers, toy shops, and pastry cooks?" Everything is going to destruction, the old trader thinks, shaking
his head as he goes through the well-known streets, where
once the fine ladies came in their fine coaches standing in two
rows; he cannot think but that trade itself is coming to an end
when such changes can come to pass. Trade, he says, like
vice, has come to a height, and as things decline when they
are at their extremes, so trade not only must decline, but does
already sensibly decline. It ought to be a comfort to the many
timid persons who have lived and prophesied evil since then to
hear that Defoe a hundred and fifty years ago had come to
this sad conclusion.

He was born into a world he thus describes, into the atmosphere of shops and counting-houses, where the good tradesman lived in the parlor above or behind his shop, and was called with a bell when need was, and was constant at business "from seven in the morning till twelve, and from two to nine at night," the interval being occupied with dinner; where the appearance of the long, flowing periwig and the sword and the man in blue livery were the danger-signals, and showed that he must break, he could not hold; where the cry of "Stop, thief!" might suddenly get up in the midst of the traffic, and the constable be called to some fainting fine lady who had got a piece of taffeta or a lace in her muff or under her hoop; and where, perhaps the greatest risk of all, a young man of genius, who was but a hosier, might betray himself in a coffee-house and be visited afterward by great personages veiling their lace and embroidery under their cloaks, who wanted a seasonable pamphlet or a newspaper put into the right way. A strange old London, more difficult to put on record in its manners and features than it is to record in pasteboard its outward aspect; where town could be convulsed by a chance broadsheet, and the Government propped or wounded to death by an anonymous essayist; when men of letters were secretaries of state, and other men of letters starved in Grub street, and the masses thanked God they could not read; when a revolution was made for liberty of conscience, yet every office and privilege was barred by a test, and intolerance was the habit of the time. The author of "Robinson Crusoe" must have got all his ideas in the narrow, bustling streets, full of rumors, of wars and commotions, and talk about the scandals of the court, and sight of the finery and license which revolted, yet exercised some strange fascinations upon the sober dissenting tradesmen who had found the sway of Oliver a hard one. He was born the year after the Restoration, and was no doubt carried out of London post-haste with the rest of his family in the early summer when the roads were crowded with wagons and carts full of women, children, and servants, all flying from the plague. The butcher's little son was but four, but very likely retained a recollection of the crowded ways and strange spectacles of the time; and no doubt he saw, with eyes starting out of their little sockets with excitement and terror, the glare of the great fire which burned down all the haunts of the pestilence and cured London by destroying it. Then, both at school, at Newington, and in the parlor behind the shop, there would be many a grave talk over what was to come of all the wickedness in high places; and when the papist king came to the throne, many discussions as to how much his new-born liberality was good for, and whether there was any safety in trusting to his indulgences and declarations of liberty of conscience. Defoe by this time was old enough to speak his own mind. He had left school at nineteen, and till he was twenty-four there is no appearance that he was doing anything, save, perhaps, picking up notions on trade in general, and as much as a young dissenter could, among his own class, or in the coffee-houses where it was safe, delivering his sentiments upon questions so vital to the welfare of the country. According to his own statement, he had written a pamphlet in 1683 to prove that a Christian power, though popish, was better than the Turk. He was now so bold as to tell the dissenters " he had rather the Church of England should pull our clothes off by fines and forfeitures than the papists should fall both upon the church and the dissenters, and pull our skins off by fire and faggot." No doubt he was then about in London noticing everything, discoursing largely with a wonderful, long-winded, sober enthusiasm, making every statement that occurred to him look like the most certain truth; talking everywhere, in the coffee-house, at the street corners, down in Cripplegate in the paternal parlor, never silent; a swarthy youth, with quick gray eyes and keen, eager features,

DANIEL DEFOE.

ENGRAVED BY C. A. POWELL, AFTER COPPERPLATE BY M. VAN DER GUCHT,
IN THE BRITISH MUSEUM.

and large, loquacious mouth. Better be fined and silenced than
let in popery to burn you into the bargain. Better stand fast
in all those deprivations and hold your faith in corners, than
accept suspicious favor from such a source, and help to bring in
again the Jesuit and the Pope. While Penn, with his plausible
speech and amiable temper, drew his Quaker brethren into a
strange harmony with the courtier's arts, and presented addresses to James, and accepted his grace, the young tradesman
would be pressing his very different argument upon the suspicious somber groups far from St. James's, where there was no
finery, but a great deal of determination. And when in the
disturbed and confused wretchedness of the time, no man knowing what was about to happen, but sure that some change
must come, young Monmouth set up his hapless standard,
could it be Defoe's own impulse, or the catch of some eddy of
feeling into which he had been swept, which carried him off
into the ranks of the adventurer? It is said that three of his
fellow-students at Newington figure among the victims of the
Bloody Assize. Defoe would always be more disposed to talk
than fight. He must, we cannot help thinking, have thought
it a feeble proceeding to put yourself in the way of getting
your head cut off, when you could use it so much more effectu-
ally in convincing your fellow-creatures. His mind, ever so
ready to slip through every loophole, carried his body off
safely out of the clutches of Jeffreys. Probably when he turned
up at home against all hope after this unlucky escapade, his
friends were too thankful to thrust him into the hosier's ware-
house, where no doubt he would give himself the air of having
sold and bought hose all his life.

There is, however, nothing to build any account of his life
upon in these earlier years. The revolution filled him with
enthusiasm, and King William gained his full and honest support — a support both bold and serviceable, and with nothing in

it which was not to his credit. But apparently a man cannot be so good a talker, so active a politician, and follow the rules which he himself laid down for a successful tradesman at the same time. Most likely his mind was never in his hose, and the world was full of so many more exciting matters. Seven years after he had been set up in business he "broke," and had to fly, though no further than Bristol, apparently, where he made an arrangement with his creditors. He would seem to have failed for the large sum at that time of seventeen thousand pounds, which he honestly exerted himself to pay, and so far succeeded in doing so that he reduced in a few years his debts to five thousand pounds in all; and, what was still more, finding certain of the creditors with whom he had compounded to be poor, after he had paid his composition fully, he made up to them the entire amount of his debt—an unlooked-for and exceptional example of honorable sentiment. Some years later, when Defoe had got into notoriety, and was the object of a great deal of violent criticism, a contemporary gives this fact, on the authority indeed of an anonymous gentleman in a coffee-house only, but it seems to have been generally received as true. The writer was in a company "where I and everybody else were railing at him," when "the gentleman took us up with this short speech:

"'Gentlemen,' said he, 'I know this Defoe as well as any of you, for I was one of his creditors, compounded with him and discharged him fully. Several years afterward he sent for me, and, though he was clearly discharged, he paid me all the remainder of his debt, voluntarily and of his own accord, and he told me that, as far as God should enable him, he intended to do so with everybody. When he had done he desired me to set my hand to a paper to acknowledge it, which I readily did, and found a great many names to the paper before me, and I think myself bound to own it.'"

This has a suspicious resemblance to Defoe's own style, but the fact seems to be generally received as true.

Neither his business nor his failure, however, kept him from the active exercise of his literary powers, which he used in the service of King William with what seems to have been a most genuine and hearty sympathy. Pamphlet after pamphlet came from his pen with an influence upon public opinion which it is difficult to estimate nowadays, but which was certainly much greater than any fugitive political publications could have now. He wrote in defense of a standing army, the curious insular prejudice against which was naturally astonishing as well as annoying to the continental prince who had become king of Great Britain. He wrote in support of the war, which to William was a vital necessity, but which England was somewhat slow to see in the same light. And, most effectively of all, he answered the always ready national grumble against foreigners, which was especially angry and thunderous against the Dutchmen, by the triumphant doggerel of "The True-born Englishman," the first of Defoe's works which takes a conspicuous place. In this strange and not very refined production he held up to public admiration the pedigree of the race which complained so warmly of every new invasion, and held so high an opinion of itself. "A true-born Englishman 's a contradiction," he cries, and sets forth, step by step, the admixtures of new blood which have gone to the formation of the English people — Roman, Saxon, Dane, Norman.

> From this amphibious, ill-born mob began
> That vain, ill-natured thing, an Englishman.

It is not a very delicate hand which traces these, and many another wave of strange ancestors. "Still the ladies loved the conquerors." But Defoe's rude lines went straight to the mark. The public had no objection to a coarse touch when it was effective, and Englishmen are rarely offended by ridicule; never, we may say, when it is home-born.   The stroke was so true that the native sense of humor was hit.   Perhaps England did not, on account of Defoe's verses, like the Dutchmen any better, but she acknowledged Tutchin's seditious assault upon the foreigners to be fully answered, and the universal laugh cleared the air.   Eighty thousand copies of this publication were sold, it is said, in the streets, where everybody bought the "lampoon," which, assailing everybody, gave no individual sting.   It also procured for Defoe a personal introduction to the king.   Whether it was to this or to his former services that he owed a small appointment he held for some years, it is difficult to say, but evidently he did not serve King William for nothing.   In the mean time Defoe resumed his business occupations, and set up a manufactory of pantiles at Tilbury, where he employed a hundred poor laborers, and throve, or seems to have thriven, in his new industry, living in something like luxury, and paying off, as described, his previous debts.   His head was full of the projects upon which one of his most successful pamphlets was written, and he recommended many sweeping schemes and made many bold suggestions on all subjects, from the institution of an income tax to that of an academy like the French.   It was a period when the air was swarming with schemes, and Defoe was not necessarily original in his suggestions; but his brain was teeming with life and energy, and there is no saying which was absolutely his own thought, and which the thought of others. He was a man to whom ideas came as he was writing, and were flung off into the air, to fly or fall as they might.   One thought, one fancy, suggested another.   For instance, after arguing long and well in favor of the war with France, which was the object of King William's life, and the only thing that could save —according to the ideas of his party on the Continent, and eventually of most sound Protestants in England—the Protestant faith, Defoe, with a sudden whimsical perception of certain possibilities on the other side, came out with a pamphlet entitled, "Reasons Against a War with France," which was founded on the suggestion that a war with Spain instead would be very profitable, and that the Spanish Indies were a booty well worth having: a sudden dash into new fields which must have brought up the public which he had persuaded to fight France with a certain gasp of breathless inability to follow this rapid reasoner in the instantaneous change of front, which meant no real change of opinion, but only the flash of a sudden happy thought.

When William died, however, and the times changed, the High Church came back with Anne into a potency which had been impossible in the unsympathetic reign of that Dutchman. Defoe had written some time before against the practice of occasional conformity; that is, the device by which dissenters managed to hold public offices in despite of existing tests, by kneeling now and then at the altars of the established church, and receiving the communion there. Defoe took the highest view of principle in this respect, and denounced the nonconformists who thus secured office to themselves by the sacrifice of their consciences, " bowing in the House of Rimmon." There seems no reason, in fact, why a moderate dissenter should not do this, except that any religious duty specially performed for the sake of a secular benefit is always suspect and odious. Yet the obvious argument that a man who could reconcile it with his conscience to attend the worship of the church should not be a dissenter, was unquestionably sound and unassailable in point of logic. Defoe had deeply offended the dissenters, to whom he himself belonged, by his protest; but this did not prevent him from rushing into print in defense of the expedient of occasional conformity as soon as it was threatened from the other side. There is little difficulty in following the action of his mind in such a question. It was wrong and a deflection from the highest point of duty to sacrifice one's conscience, even occasionally, for the sake of office; but, on the other hand, it was equally wrong to abolish an expedient which broke the severity of the test, and made life possible to the nonconforming classes. The views were contradictory, yet both were true, and it was his nature to see both sides with most impartial good sense, while he felt it to be, if a breach of external consistency, no wrong to defend or assail one side or the other, as might seem most necessary. He allowed himself so complete a license on this point that it is curious he should be found the public champion of the higher duty. No doubt his utterance to his dissenting brethren on that question was to himself no reason why he should not defend their right to use the expedient if they had a mind. But this is too fine a distinction for the general intelligence.

The discussions on this subject were the occasion of one of the most striking episodes in his life. When the bill against occasional conformity was introduced, to the delight of the High Church party, from the queen downward, and when the air began to buzz around him with the bluster, hitherto subdued by circumstances, of the reviving party, who would have made short work with the dissenters had their power been equal to their will, a grimly humorous perception of the capabilities of the occasion seems to have seized Defoe. Notwithstanding that he had angered all the sects by his plain speaking, he was a dissenter born, and there is no such way of reconverting a stray Israelite as to hear the Philistines blaspheme. He seized upon the extremest views of the high-fliers with characteristic insight, and, with a keen consciousness of the power of his weapon, used it remorselessly. The "Shortest Way to Deal with Dissenters" is a grave and elaborate statement of the wild threats and violent talk in which, in the intoxication of newly acquired power, the partizans of the church indulged, with noise and exaggeration proportioned to the self-suppression which had been forced upon them by the panic of a papal restoration under James, and by the domination of the more moderate party during William's unsympathetic reign. They were now at the top of the wave, and could brandish their swords in the eyes of their adversaries. Their talk in some of their public utterances was as bloodthirsty as if they intended a St. Bartholomew. Defoe took up this frenzied babble, and put it into the form of a grave and practical proposal. As serious as was Swift when he proposed to utilize the superabundant babies of the poor by eating them, Defoe propounded the easy way to get rid of the dissenters and the necessity of settling this question forever. " Shall any law be given to such wild creatures? Some beasts are for sport, and the huntsman gives them advantages of ground, but some are knocked on the head by all possible ways of violence and surprise." He says:

'T is vain to trifle in this matter. The light, foolish handling of them by mulcts, fines, etc., 't is their glory and their advantage. If the gallows instead of the counter, and the galleys instead of the fines, were the reward of going to a conventicle to preach or to hear, there would not be so many sufferers The spirit of martyrdom is over. They that will go to church to be chosen sheriffs and mayors would go to forty churches rather than be hanged. If one severe law were made and punctually executed, that whoever was found at a conventicle should be banished, the nation and the preacher be hanged, we should see an end of the tale. They would all come to church, and one age would make us all one again.

To talk of 5s. a month for not coming to this sacrament, and 1s. per week for not coming to church, this is such a way of converting people as never was known. This is selling them a liberty to transgress for so much money. If it be not a crime, why don't we give them full license? And if it be, no price ought to compound for committing it, for that is selling a liberty to people to sin against God and the government.

If it be a crime of the highest consequence, both against the peace and welfare of the nation, the glory of God, the good of the church, and the happiness of the soul, let us rank it among capital offences, and let it receive a punishment in proportion to it.

We hang men for trifles and banish them for things not worth naming. But an offence against God and the church, against the welfare of the world, and the dignity of religion shall be bought off for 5s.—this is such a shame to a Christian Government that 't is with regret I transmit it to posterity.

If men sin against God, affront his ordinances, rebel against his church, and disobey the precepts of their superiors, let them suffer as such capital crimes deserve: so will religion flourish, and this divided nation be once again united. . . . I am not supposing that all the dissenters in England should be hanged or banished, but as in cases of rebellions and insurrections, if a few of the ringleaders suffer, the multitude are dismissed; so a few obstinate people being bad examples, there 's no doubt but the severity of the law would find a stop in the compliance of the multitude.

The reader will perceive by what a serious argument the hot-headed fanatic was betrayed and the wiser public put upon their guard. The mirror thus held up to nature, with a grotesque twist in it which made the likeness bewildering, gave London such a sensation as she had not felt for many a day. The wildest excitement arose. At first all parties in the shock of surprise took it for genuine. "The wisest churchmen in the nation were deceived by it," and while some were even so foolish as to receive it with unthinking applause, which was the case, according to Oldmixon, "in our two famous Universities," the more sensible reader of the church party was first indignant with the high-flyers for expressing such opinions, and then furious with the satirist who had insulted the church by putting them into her mouth. Nobody indeed saw the joke. The fellow of Cambridge who thanked his bookseller for packing up "so excellent a treatise" along with the books he had ordered, and considered it "next to the Sacred Bible and Holy Comments the best book he ever saw"; the "soberer churchman" who "openly exclaimed against the proposal, condemned the

CHURCH OF ST. GILES, CRIPPLEGATE,
WHERE DEFOE IS SUPPOSED TO HAVE BEEN BAPTIZED.

DRAWN BY HARRY FENN. ENGRAVED BY H. E. SYLVESTER.

warmth that appeared in the clergy, and openly professed that such a man as Sacheverell and his brethren would blow up the foundations of the church"; the dissenters who were at once insulted and alarmed by the extraordinary threats thus set forth against them—all alike turned upon the perpetrator of the hoax when he was discovered. Some "blushed when they reflected how far they had applauded," some labored to prove that it was "a horrible slander against the church." The government, sharing the general commotion, placed Defoe in the position of a revolutionary leader who, "by the villainous insinuations of that pamphlet, would have frightened the dissenters into another rebellion." Defoe himself seems to have had a moment of panic, and fled. He was proclaimed in the "Gazette," and a reward offered for his discovery. His biographers in general assert that he gave himself up with some generosity to save the printer and publisher, who had been arrested, but there are public documents which seem to prove a different procedure, showing how "My Lord Nottingham hunted him out," and how "the person who discovered Daniel Foe" claimed and was paid the reward of fifty pounds offered for the offender, described as a "middle-aged, spare man, about forty years old, of a brown complexion and dark brown colored hair (but wears a wig), a hooked nose, a sharp chin, gray eyes, and a large mole near his mouth." However that might be, he was arrested and committed to Newgate in the spring of 1703, and the obnoxious publication—"this little book, a contemptible pamphlet of but three sheets of paper," as he describes it—was burned by the common hangman. It was not, however, till the summer, three or four months after his arrest, that he was tried, and that period he seems to have spent in Newgate in perfect freedom, at least for literary productions, since he filled the air with a mist of pamphlets explaining that he meant nothing but a harmless satire at one moment, at another exhorting the dis-

senters to be content with spiritual freedom, and again bursting
into the rude but potent strains of the "Hymn to the Pillory."
He was sentenced to fine and imprisonment, as well as to that
grotesque but sometimes terrible instrument of torture; but the
pillory was no torture to Defoe.   On the last three days of
July — once before the Royal Exchange in Cornhill, where his
shop had been, and where no doubt everybody knew him, once
in Cheapside, and again at Temple Bar — he stood aloft with
the crowd surging round and performed his penance.   The
crowd in those days was not a soft or civil one when it indorsed
the sentence pronounced by law.   Its howls and cries, its mis-
siles and its curses, made the punishment horrible.   But the
crowd had by this time found time to take in the joke, — banter,
when it is broad enough to be intelligible, always pleases the
general, — and there must have been some bonhomie about the
sufferer, some good repute as a merry fellow and one who
loved a jest, which conciliated the populace.   Instead of dead
cats, they flung him nosegays; they gathered about his platform
under the low deep arch which once made a mock gate to the
city, and behind the bustling 'Change, and between the shops
of Cheapside, holding a series of impromptu festivals, drinking
his health, shouting out his new verses, which were sold by
thousands in the streets:

> Hail, hieroglyphic state machine,
> Contriv'd to punish fancy in;
> Men that are men, in thee can feel no pain,
> And all thy insignificants disdain;
> Exalted on thy stool of state,
> What prospect do I see of sovereign fate.

The bold satirist, looking through those "lofty loops," re-
calls all the good men that have stood there, reminding himself
that even the learned Selden had the pillory in prospect, and
that, had he "triumphed on thy stage," no man could have

shunned it more. Contempt, "that false new word for shame," has no power where there is no crime, he declares. The lines are rough, but the sentiments are manly and full of honest scorn, which here and there reaches a high tone. From his platform where he stood in all the emancipation of feeling that the worst had happened, he throws a bold glance upon the disorders of the time, political and social, and summons to this post of scorn the firebrands, the cowards, the failures of the age. One can imagine those keen gray eyes inspecting through the loops the hoarse and roaming groups, not sure perhaps what his reception was to be, gathering courage as the shouts became intelligible and turned into hurrahs for Defoe. No doubt he marked the fluctuating 'crowd as keenly as if he had been a careless spectator at a window, and saw Colonel Jack and his brother pickpockets threading devious ways among the multitude, with here and there a gallant from St. James in his long curled periwig fluttering on the edge, and the tradesmen, half curious, half unwilling to join in the riot, looking on from their doors. A pillory is a coign of vantage when the man upon it has eyes like Defoe's. "Tell 'em," he says, apostrophizing his platform contemptuously—

> Tell 'em the men that placed him here
> Are friends unto the times,
> But at a loss to find his guilt,
> They can't commit his crimes.

Mr. Burton, in his "Reign of Queen Anne," quotes from manuscript authority a statement that Penn had been commissioned by Defoe to offer " an account of all his accomplices in whatsoever he has been concerned," on condition that he should be freed from the pillory, which is a very confusing statement, since it seems impossible to understand what accomplices he could have had. This, according to the same authority, was considered important enough to call for a special meeting of the cabinet council; but "the Queen seems to think that his confession amounts to nothing." Another account is that Nottingham visited him in prison and offered him his liberty if he would say who set him on to do it. Thus this *jeu d'esprit*—the first exercise of Defoe's special and most characteristic gift, that of endowing a fictitious production with every appearance of reality—set the world aflame. It is almost a more astonishing feat than the narratives which look so like literal transcripts of experience; for the subtle power which, by a cunning fitting together of actual utterances, could thus indicate the alarming tendency and danger of a great party, is more wonderful than to create an imaginary man and trace his every action as if he were a real one. The art may be less noble, but it is more difficult. Indeed, the "Shortest Way" is about the only example of such an extraordinary achievement. Swift's tremendous satire was more bitter, more scathing, and treated not so much the exaggerated opinions of a class as the cruel and callous indifference of human nature to the sufferings of its slaves and victims.

This curious episode once more ruined Defoe. It is to be supposed that when he went into hiding his business had to be abandoned, and all his affairs got into confusion. The official document already quoted describes him as "living at Newington Green with his father-in-law, who is a lay elder of a conventicle there." This description, however, is evidently drawn up by an enemy, since his previous bankruptcy is spoken of as fraudulent, an assertion made nowhere else. His biographer, Wilson, informs us that though he had "kept his coach" before this period, the pantile works had now to be broken up, and his business was ruined. He had, though there is no information about her, a wife and six children—perhaps supported by the elder at Newington, who very likely thought, like his brethren, but badly of Defoe.

He lay in Newgate for nearly a year, without, however, to all appearance, losing any opportunity for a pamphlet during the whole time, and laying in grist for his mill amid the strange and terrible surroundings of an eighteenth-century prison. Mr. Minto, in the admirable sketch of Defoe which he has contributed to the "English Men of Letters" series, seems to think that his hero must have enjoyed himself in this teeming world of new experiences, and that "he spent many pleasant hours" listening to the tales of his fellow-prisoners. No doubt there must have been some compensation to such a man in making acquaintance with a new aspect of life, but it is, perhaps, going too far to attribute a possibility of enjoyment to any undegraded man in the pandemonium described in so many contemporary narratives. Defoe did, however what, so far as we are aware, no other man before or after him has ever done (except, perhaps, Leigh Hunt, in whose case we have a vague recollection of similar activity): he originated, wrote, and published a newspaper in his prison. "The Review," so called, "of the Affairs of France"— that is, of the affairs of Europe and the world— that is, of any political subject that might be uppermost—was published twice a week, and appeared during the whole time of his imprisonment. A brilliant, familiar, graphic commentary upon all that was happening, a dialogue between the imprisoned spectator of life and the busy world outside, in which he was both questioner and answerer, pouring out upon the country with the keenest understanding of other people's views, and the most complete mastery of his own, his remarks and criticisms, his judgment and advice. A newspaper in those days was not, of course, the huge broadsheet which it has now become. The "Review" was a sheet of eight, but afterward of only four small quarto pages. It was no assemblage of paragraphs, trivial or important, the work of many anonymous persons whose profession it is to manufacture a newspaper, but one

10*

man's eager and lively conversation with his countrymen, full
of the vigor of personal opinion and the unity of an individual
view.   A keener intelligence was never brought to the treatment of public affairs, nor a mind more thoughtful, reasonable,
and practical.   His prejudices were few — too few, perhaps.
Granted that the aim was good, Defoe was disdainful of punc-
tilio in the way of carrying it out.   He was not above doing
evil that good might come, but he had a far higher refinement
of meaning than could be embraced by any such vulgar statement in his subtle faculty of discovering, and all but proving,
that what might have seemed evil to a common intelligence was
in reality a good, if not the best, way of carrying his excellent
purpose out.   Up to the moment of his leaving Newgate, however, there was nothing equivocal in the use he made of his extraordinary faculties.   He was a free man discussing boldly on
his own responsibility, and without any *arrière pensée*, the affairs
of England.   If he had first keenly assailed the dissenters, who
were his own people, in respect of the compliances by which they
made themselves capable of bearing office, and then exposed to
grimmest ridicule the adversaries who aimed at rendering them
altogether incapable, there was in this no real inconsistency.
His championship of King William had been honest and thor-
ough.   If he loved to have a finger in every pie, and let loose
his opinion at every crisis, there was no contemporary opinion
which was better worth having.   But now this unwearying
critic, this keen observer, this restless, brilliant casuist, this
practical man of business, had come to the turning-point of
his life.

His liberation from Newgate followed closely upon the ad-
vent of Harley to power.   When this event happened, it is said
that one of the first things the new minister did was to send a
message to Defoe in prison : " Pray ask that gentleman what I
can do for him."   Whether it was in direct sequence to this

question, or whether the Queen had formed an independent intention of freeing the prisoner, we need not inquire; but he was set free, Queen Anne furnishing the means of paying his fine. She is said also to have taken an interest in his family, and contributed to their support during his confinement. He declared himself to be liberated on the condition of writing nothing (further modified as nothing " which some people might not like ") for some years; a condition which he immediately fulfilled by publishing an " Elegy on the Author of the True-born Englishman," to tell the world so, and took no further notice of the prohibition, so far as appears. The real meaning of this curious statement would seem by all evidence to have been that Defoe there and then accepted the position of a secret servant of the government, a writer pledged to support their measures and carry out their views. At the moment, and perhaps in reality during the greater part of his career, their measures were those which he approved; and certainly at this period of his history he has never been accused of writing against his conscience. Even when, after eager championship of peace, he was obliged by political changes to veer into what looked like support of war, he was never without the strong defense to fall back upon, that he demanded peace only after securing certain indispensable conditions, and that war might be, and was, the only means of gaining them — an argument most simple and evident to his mind.

Harley has never appeared in history as a great man, but when we consider that he was able thus to subjugate and secure to his own service two of the greatest intelligences of his time, it is impossible not to respect his influence and judgment. The great and somber genius of Swift, the daring, brilliant, and ever-ready intellect of Defoe, became instruments in the hands of this ordinary and scheming statesman. Once more, with a curious parallelism, these two men stand before us — no friends

to each other. "An illiterate fellow, whose name I forget," says
Swift, with the almost brutal scorn which was part of his character; while Defoe replies to the taunt with angry virulence, setting forth his own acquirements, "though he wrote no bill at
his door, nor set Latin on the front of his productions," a piece
of pretension, habitual to the time, of which the other was guilty.
But Harley, who was not worthy, so far as intellect went, to
clean the shoes of either, had them both at his command, serving his purposes, doing his bidding. Which of them suffered
most by the connection it is not easy to say. It turned Swift's
head, and brought into humiliating demonstration the braggart
and the bully in his nature. Defoe had not the demoralizing
chance of being the lord treasurer's boon companion; but
Harley made a dishonest partizan, a paid and slippery special
pleader and secret agent, out of the free-lance of politics.
From this moment the defenders and champions of Defoe have
to turn into casuists, as he himself did. They have to give
specious explanations to suppress and account for his shifts and
changes, though at first they were sufficiently innocent. The
evil grew, however, so that toward the end of his career even
the apologist must keep silence; but this is the nature of all
evil.

If excuses are to be sought for Defoe's conduct in this first
beginning of his slavery, it will not be difficult to find them. The
age, for one thing, was corrupt through and through. There was
not a statesman but had two strings to his bow, nor a politician
of any description who did not attempt to serve two masters.
To hold the balance between Hanover and St.-Germain, ready
to perform a demi-volt in the air at any moment as the scale
should turn, was the science of the day. On the other hand, Defoe was now a ruined man, with a family to support, and nothing
but his busy and inexhaustible pen to do it with. The material
inducement of a certain income to fall back upon, whatever

ROBERT HARLEY, EARL OF OXFORD.

ENGRAVED BY JOHN P. DAVIS, AFTER THE ORIGINAL PAINTING BY
SIR GODFREY KNELLER, IN THE BRITISH MUSEUM.

might be the chances of journalism, must have been very strong. And what was stronger still was the delight of his own vivacious, restless, ready mind, with its sense of boundless power and infinite resource, to which difficulty was a delight and the exercise of walking over hot coals or dancing on a sword-point the most exhilarating possibility, in making its triumphant way over obstacles which would have baffled almost all his contemporaries. "The danger's self was lure alone" to this skilled and cunning fencer, this master of all the arts. In a very different sense from that of Tennyson's noble hero, "Faith Unfaithful" was inspiration and strength to him, and to be falsely true the most delightful situation. He loved to support his principles by a hundred dodges, and plead them from the other side, and make of himself the devil's advocate in the interest of heaven. All this was life to his mind. He must have had a positive pleasure in proving to himself first, and then to all England, that the happiest thing a Whig could do was to find the Tory measures exactly those which he would have recommended, and that his allegiance to the queen required a change of policy on his part whenever circumstances compelled her to change her ministry. It was all devotion — not time-serving, as the vulgar thought. Defoe took infinite pleasure in proving that it was so, in making everything clear. The commonplace and humdrum expedient of following your party would have been dull to him — a proceeding without interest as without danger. He wanted excitement, obstacles to get over; a position which would make sudden claims upon his ingenuity to account for and fortify it. Such a mind is rare, and still more rarely is it accompanied by genius. But when such a combination does occur it is a very curious spectacle.

In the mean time, however, all that Defoe had to do was simple enough. He had to support peace and the union — two things which in his free estate he had already advocated

with all his powers. He did it with the utmost skill, fervor, and
success, and to all appearance contributed much to the great
public act which was the subject of so many struggles and re-
sistances on the part of the smaller nation — the union. This
great expedient, of which from the first he had seen the advantage, Defoe worked for with unwearying zeal. He praised and
caressed Caledonia — upon which subject he wrote one of those
vigorous essays in verse which he called poetry — and the tol-
erance of the Presbyterian Church, and the good sense of the
nation generally, which was not always perceptible to English
politicians; and even risked a visit to Edinburgh in performance of the orders of the government, though at the risk of
rude handling to himself. In all this there cannot be the slightest doubt that he was entirely honest and patriotic, and acted
from an enlightened personal view of the necessities of the case.
When the curious incident of the Sacheverell prosecution occurred, he had once more a subject entirely to his own mind,
and expressed his own feelings in supporting with all his might
the measures of the government against that High Church fire-
brand, one of the chief of those whom he had held up to public
ridicule in the "Shortest Way." So far he was fortunate, being
employed upon subjects entirely congenial to his mind, and on
which he had already strong convictions. The equivocal part
of the matter is that he never ceased to assert and insist upon
his independence. "Contemn," he says, "as not worth men-
tioning, the suggestions of some people of my being employed
to carry on the interests of a party. I have never loved any
party, but with my utmost zeal have sincerely espoused the
great and original interest of this nation and of all nations — I
mean truth and liberty"—which was the truth, yet not all the
truth. Again, with still more violent protestations, he refers to
his private circumstances, of which nothing is known, to prove
how little he was protected by power. It would seem from this

statement that he was still being pursued for the remnant of old debts, or those new ones with which the failure of his tile factory and his long imprisonment had saddled him.

> If paid, gentlemen, for writing [he cries], if hired, if employed, why still harassed with merciless and malicious men ; why pursued to all extremities of law for old accounts which you clear other men of every day ? Why oppressed, distressed, and driven from his family, and from all his prospects of delivering them and himself? Is this the fate of men employed and hired ? Is this the figure the agents of courts and princes make ?

The argument is a feeble one for such a practised reasoner as Defoe, without considering the trifling detail that it was untrue, for debts are by no means unknown to favorites of the crown. Nor could he have been saved by Harley's pay, which probably was never very great, from the consequences of previous misfortunes. The reader will think that a judicious silence would have been more appropriate, but that was not Defoe's way. The only wonder is that he did not adduce such detailed evidence of his own freedom as would have deceived any man, and shown to demonstration that it was he who subsidized the ministry, and not they him. The wonderful thing is that he was free through all, maintaining his own favorite opinions, working as an independent power. Servile journalists have existed in plenty, but seldom one who took the pay of his masters and served their interests, yet fought under his own flag with honesty and a good conscience all the while.

This happy state, however, did not last. Harley fell, but with his last breath (as a minister) adjured his champion not to sacrifice himself, but to come to an understanding with his successor, Godolphin. This necessitated a certain revolution in respect to peace, which Defoe managed cleverly with the excellent device above mentioned. And there was still higher ground which he felt himself entitled to take. The public safety was involved in the stability of the new ministry such as it was. And he faces the dilemma with boundless pluck and assurance. "Though I don't like the crew, I won't sink the ship; I 'll pump and heave and haul and do everything I can, though he that pulls with me were my enemy. The reason is plain. We are all in the ship and must sink or swim together." These admirable reasonings brought him at last to the calm rectitude of the following conclusion:

It occurred to me instantly as a principle for my conduct that it was not material to me what ministers her Majesty was pleased to employ. My duty was to go along with every ministry so far as they did not break in upon the constitution and the laws and liberties of my country, my part being only the duty of a subject, viz: to submit to all lawful commands, and to enter into no service that was not justifiable by the laws, to all of which I have exactly obliged myself.

When Harley returned to power, another modification became necessary, but Defoe piously felt it was providential that he should thus be thrown back upon his original protector; and had the matter ended here, as was long supposed, it is difficult to see what indictment could be brought against him. It is not expedient certainly that a director of public opinion should have state pay, and does not look well when the secret is betrayed. But so long as the scope of all his productions is good, honest, and patriotic, with only as much submission in trifles as is inevitable, the bargain is a personal meanness rather than a public crime, and this was long supposed to have been the case. It was believed that after the death of Queen Anne and Harley's final fall, Defoe's eloquent mouth was closed, and he disappeared into the calm of private life to earn a better hire and a more lasting influence through the two immortal works of fiction by which alone, but for the painful labors of biographers, his name would have been known. Had the matter been left so, how much happier would it have been for the hero of this romance

of literary life, how much more edifying for posterity! We could
have imagined the tired warrior retiring from that hot and painful field in which even the laurels were not worth the plucking,
where defeat was miserable and success mean, and scarcely any
combatant could keep his honor intact, to the quietness of
some suburban house in which his three pretty daughters could
care for him and idolize him, and where his wonderful imagination, no longer a slave to the exigencies of political warfare,
could weave its dreams into a sober certainty of life awake.
We should then have said of the author of " Robinson Crusoe "
and the " Journal of the Plague," that in his poverty and anxiety and overhaste he had been beguiled into a bargain which
might have been a shameful one had not his marvelous power
of seeing every side of a subject, and that insight of genius
which divines the real unity of honest souls through all the external diversities which fill the limited vision of common men,
carried him triumphantly through. And upon what real fault
there was we should have thrown a veil. The age would have
borne the blame—an age which was corrupt to the core, and in
which men changed their principles every day. In the garden
at Newington, where the young ladies entertained their lovers,
we could have pictured him benevolent and friendly in the flowing peruke under which his keen eyes sparkled, looking on
at the love-making with prudent, tradesmanlike thoughts of
Sophia's portion, and how much the young people would have
to set up housekeeping upon, coming in not inappropriately
between the pages of Crusoe—perhaps taking a suggestion
about Robinson's larder from some passing talk about the store-
room, or modifying for the use of Friday some rustical remark
of the young serving-man from the country, or in the renewing
of old recollections produced by some old friend's visit finding
an anecdote, a detail, to incorporate into the "Journal of the
Plague." And we should have asked ourselves by what strange

play of genius the unenchanted island, where all the sober elaborations of fact clothed so completely the vivid realizations of imagination, should have risen out of the mists amid those trim, old-fashioned alleys, and green plots, and stiff parterres of flowers.

Alas! That demon of research which in its poking and prying sometimes puts old bones together, and sometimes scatters to the winds the ashes of the dead, has spoiled this pleasant picture. Impelled by its influence, an unwary or else too painstaking student, some twenty years ago, was seized with the idea of roaming the earth in search of relics of Defoe. And the diabolical powers which put this fatal pursuit into his mind directed him to a bundle of yellow papers in the State Paper Office which has, alas! for ever and ever made an end of our man of genius. These treacherous papers give us to wit under his own hand that he was in reality in full action in the most traitorous of employments during the period of his supposed retirement. The following, which is the first of these fatally self-elucidatory letters, will reveal at once the inconceivable occupation to which Defoe in his downfall lent himself. He had perhaps compromised himself too much, and been too completely identified with Harley at the end to be considered capable of more honorable and evident employment. The letter is addressed to the secretary of the minister who had given him his disgraceful office:

It was proposed by my Lord Townsend that I should appear as if I were as before under the displeasure of the government, and separated from the Whigs, and that I might be more serviceable in a kind of disguise than if I appeared openly. In the interval of this, Dyer, the "News-Letter" writer, being dead, and Dormer, his successor, being unable by his troubles to carry on that work, I had an offer of a share in the property as well as in the management of that work.

I immediately acquainted my Lord Townsend of it, who, by Mr. Buckley, let me know it would be a very acceptable piece of service, for that letter was really very prejudicial to the public, and the most difficult to come at in a judicial way in case of offense given. My Lord was pleased to add, by Mr. Buckley, that he would consider my service in that case, as he afterwards did.

Upon this I engaged in it, and that so far, that though the property was not wholly my own, yet the conduct and government of the style of news was so entirely in me, that I ventured to assure His Lordship the sting of that mischievous paper should be entirely taken out, though it was granted that the style should continue Tory, as it was, that the party might be amused and not set up another, which would have destroyed the design, and this part I therefore take entirely on myself still.

This went on for a year before my Lord Townsend went out of the office, and His Lordship, in consideration of the service, made me the appointment which Mr. Buckley knows of, with promise of a further allowance as service presented.

My Lord Sunderland, to whose goodness I had many years ago been obliged, when I was in a secret commission sent to Scotland, was pleased to approve and continue this service, and the appointment annexed, and, with His Lordship's approbation I introduced myself, in the disguise of a translator of the foreign news, to be so far concerned in this weekly paper of Mist's as to be able to keep it within the circle of a secret management, also prevent the mischievous part of it, and yet neither Mist, or any of those concerned with him, have the least guess or suspicion by whose direction I do it.

There is nothing, it seems to us, for any apologist to say in explanation of this extraordinary statement. The emissary of a Whig and Hanoverian government acting as editor of a Tory and Jacobite newspaper,—nay, of three newspapers,—in order to take the harm out of them, to amuse the Tory party with a pretense of style and subjects suitable to their views, while balking all their purposes, is at once the most ingenious and the most shameless of all devices. It continued for a long period, and was very successful. But when the deceit was discovered at last, Mist, the deluded publisher, made a murderous assault upon the deceiver, and the journalists of the period seem to have risen unanimously against him. That Defoe must have

fallen sadly before he came to this is very evident; but how
he fell, except by the natural vengeance of deterioration, which
makes a man who has long paltered with the truth unable at
last to distinguish the gradations which separate the doubtful
from the criminal, no one can say.   He must, however, have
fallen indeed in position and importance before he could be put
to such miserable work; and he must have fallen more fatally,
like that other son of the morning, deep down into hades,
where he became the father of lies and the betrayer of mankind, before he could have been capable of this infamous
mission.

We turn with relief to the work which, of all these manifold
labors, is the only portion which has really survived the effects
of time.   Defoe's political writings, with all their lucidity, their
brilliant good sense, daring satire, and astonishing readiness and variety, are for the student, and retain a place among
the materials of history, studied no longer for their own sake,
but for the elucidations they may give.   But "Robinson
Crusoe" lives by his own right, and will, we may confidently
affirm, after the long trial he has had, never die.   We need
not discuss the other works of fiction which are all as characteristic as distinct narratives of apparent fact, as carefully
elaborated in every detail.   They are almost all excellent in
their beginning, but, a fault which is shared by Crusoe himself,
run into such a prodigality of detail toward their close, that
the absence of dramatic construction and of any real inspiration
of art, becomes painfully (or rather tediously, which is worse)
apparent.   We do not, however, share the opinion of those
critics who disparage Defoe's marvelous power of narrative.
"The little art he is truly master of, of forging a story and
imposing it on the world for truth," is an art which he possesses in common with but very few who have ever lived; and
even among these few he has it in a very high degree.

The gift is peculiar; we are not moved by it to pity or tenderness, and not much to admiration of the hero. The inner circle of our emotions is seldom, if ever, entered; but, on the other hand, there is nothing in that island where the shipwrecked mariner finds a shelter, and which he makes into a home, which we do not know and see, as well as if we had dwelt in it like Robinson. It is an island which is added to the geography of the world. Not only would no child ever doubt of its existence, but to the most experienced reader it is far more true and real than half of those of which we have authentic histories, which our relatives and countrymen have visited and colonized. Those South Sea Islands, about which we have so many flowery volumes, are not half so certain. And every detail of the life of its solitary inhabitant comes up before us like our own personal proceedings — more than visible, incontestable experiences. Not one of us but could draw the picture of the solitary in his furs, with all his odd implements about him; and, more wonderful still, not a child from four upward but could tell who it was. The tale does not move us as do imaginative histories on a more poetic level; but in its humbler range it is as living as the best. And there is something in this very absence of emotion which gives a still more wonderful force to the tale. Men in such desperate circumstances driven to the use of all their faculties for the mere preservation of their lives, have presumably but little time for feeling. The absorption of every faculty in this one primitive need brings a certain serenity, a calm which is like the hush of the solitude — the silence of the seas. The atmosphere is full of this stillness. There is the repose of Nature, not filled with reflections of human sentiment, but imposing her patience, her calm repetition of endless endeavor upon the solitary flung into her bosom; and there is a sobriety in the story which adds immensely to the power. Other unknown islands have

been in fiction, but none where the progress of events was so
gradual, where there were so few miraculous accessories.   One
of the most able of English romancers, the late Charles Reade,
is the last who has carried us to a desolate island.   His story
is full of charm, of humor, and sentiment far beyond the reach
of Defoe.   Nothing could be more tender, more delightful, than
the idyl of the two lovers cut off from all mankind, lost in the
silence of the seas.   But in every way his isle is an enchanted
isle.   Not only is it peopled with love and all the graces, but
it is running over with every convenience,—everything that is
useful and beautiful.   The inexhaustible ingenuity of the lover
is not more remarkable than the wealth of necessary articles of
every kind that turns up at every step.   He builds his lady a
bower lined with mother-of-pearl; he clothes her in a cloak of
sealskin; he finds jewels for her; she has but to wish and to
have, as if Regent street had been within reach.   Very different
is the sober sanity of the elder narrative.   Defoe knows nothing about lovers; all his heroes marry with prodigality; but he
has no love, any more than he has pearls or gutta-percha, on
his island.   Conveniences come very slowly to Robinson Crusoe;
he has to grope his way, and find his living hardly, patiently.
Day after day, and year after year, the story-teller goes on
working out the order of events.   It is as leisurely as nature,
as little helped by accident, as sober even as matter of fact, and
yet what a potent, clear, all-realizing fancy—a faculty which in
its limited sphere saw and felt and acted in completest appro-
priation of the circumstances — this sober imagination was !

He was fifty-eight at the time this book was written — a man
worn with endless work and strife, but ever ready for more — a
man who had fallen and failed, and made but little of his life.   It
is said that he was at his highest point of external prosperity
when he published " Robinson Crusoe"; but when we remember
that he was at that time engaged in the inconceivable muddle of

" Mist's Journal," it seems almost impossible to believe this, or to understand how anything but poverty could drive him into such a disgraceful employment. No doubt, to a man who at heart had once been an honest man, and was so no more, it must have been a relief and blessed deliverance to escape away into the distant seas, to refresh his ever-active soul with the ingenious devices of the shipwrecked sailor, and bury himself in that life so different from his own, the savage necessities, the primitive cares. The goats and the parrot and poor Friday : what an ease and comfort to escape into their society after bamboozling Mist, and reporting to my lord at St. James's ! Was it a desperate expedient of nature to save him from utter self-contempt? Such a man, even if his conscience had grown callous, must have required some outlet from the dreadful slavery to which he had bound himself.

"Robinson Crusoe" is the work by which Defoe is best known, which is, after all, the most effectual guarantee that it is his best work. But it is not, to our thinking, worthy of being placed in competition with the " Journal of the Plague"—a history so real, so solemn and impressive, so full of the atmosphere and sentiment of the time, that it reaches a far higher point of literary art than anything else Defoe has written. For this is not prose alone, nor that art of making fiction look like truth, which is supposed to be his greatest excellence : it is one of the most impressive pictures of a historical incident which has struck the poetic imagination everywhere, and of which we have perhaps more authentic records than of any other historical episode. Neither Boccaccio nor Manzoni have equaled Defoe in the story of the plague. To the old Italian it was a horror from which the life-loving fled with loathing as well as fear, and which they tried to forget and put out of their sight. Defoe's minute description of the argument carried on within his own mind by the narrator is curiously characteristic of the tendency to elaborate and explain which enters so largely into all his works. The mental condition of the respectable citizen, divided between concern for his life and concern for his property, seeing with reasonable eyes that death was not certain, but that in case of flight ruin was,—moved by the divination which he uses in all good faith, yet perhaps not with sufficient devoutness to have allowed himself to be guided by it had it been contrary to his previous dispositions, and at bottom by a certain *vis inertiæ* and disinclination to move, which is clearly indicated from the beginning,—is in his best manner, and so real that it is impossible to resist its air of absolute truthfulness. But the state of the shut-up streets, the dreadful sounds and sights, the brooding heat and stillness of the long and awful days, the cloud of fate that is about the doomed city, are beyond description impressive. This curious spectator of all things, this impartial yet eager looker-on, determined to see all that can be seen, prudent yet fearless, adopting every precaution, yet neglecting no means of investigation, inquiring everywhere, always with his eyes and ears open, at once a philosophical inquirer and an eager gossip, is without doubt Defoe himself. But he is also a marked figure of the time. He is like Pepys; he is almost, but for the unmistakable difference between the bourgeois and the fine gentleman, like Evelyn. He is one of the special kind of man born to illustrate that period. Pepys would have found means for some piece of junketing even in the midst of his alarm, whereas Defoe thinks of his property, when he has time to think of anything but the plague, which is a very natural modification consequent on the changes of the times. But they are at bottom the same. While, however, this central figure remains the characteristic but not elevated personage with whom we are already acquainted, the history which he records is done with a tragic force and completeness which it is impossible to surpass. In this there is nothing commonplace, no wearying monotony; the very statistics have a tragic solemnity in them; the awful unseen presence dominates everything. We scarcely breathe while we move about the streets emptied of all passers-by, or with a suspicious throng in the middle of the way keeping as far apart as possible from the houses. This is not mere prose: it is poetry in its most rare form; it is an ideal representation, in all its sober details, of one of the most tragical moments of human suffering and fate.

Nothing else that Defoe has done is on the same level. It is pitched on too high a key perhaps for the multitude. His innocent thief, "Colonel Jack," begins with a picture both amusing and touching of the curious moral denseness and confusion of a street boy; his "Cavalier" is a charming young man. But both these and all the rest of Defoe's heroes and heroines grow heavy and tedious at the end. The "Journal of the Plague" is not like them in this respect. The conclusion—the sudden surprise and delicious sense of relief, the joy which makes the passers-by stop and shake hands with one another in the streets, and the women call out from windows with tears and outcries of gladness—is sudden and overwhelming as the reality. We are caught in the growing despair, and suddenly in a moment deliverance comes. Here alone Defoe is not too long; the unexpected is brought in with a skill and force not less remarkable than that which in the previous pages has portrayed the slow growth and inevitable development of the misery. Up to this anticlimax of unlooked-for joy the calamity has grown, every new touch intensifying the awful reality. But the recovery is sudden, and told without an unnecessary word. It is the only instance in which Defoe has followed the instinct of a great artist and shown that he knew how to avail himself of the unwritten code and infallible methods of art.

We forget his shortcomings when we discuss this which is to our mind much his greatest work, and it is well that we should leave him in this disposition. He died mysteriously alone, after a period of wandering and hiding which nobody can explain. Whether he was in trouble with creditors, or with political enemies, or with the exasperated party which he had managed to outwit; whether he kept out of the way that his family might make better terms for themselves, or that he might keep the remains of his money out of the hands of an undutiful son, or a grasping son-in-law, nobody can tell. He died in remote lodgings, all alone, and his affairs were administered by a stranger, perhaps his landlady, no one knows. His domestic circumstances have been referred to during his life only in the vaguest way. He had a wife and a numerous family when he was put in the pillory; he had a wife, a son who was unkind, and three daughters at the end; but that is all we know. He died at seventy-two " of a lethargy," no doubt fallen into the feebleness and hopelessness of lonely old age; and that is all. His life overflowed with activity and business. To be doing seems to have been a necessity of his being. But he never seems to have enjoyed the importance due to his powers, and in an age when men of letters filled the highest posts never would appear to have risen above his citizen circle, his shop-keeping ways. Something in the man must have accounted for this, but it is difficult to say what it was; for the age did not require a high standard of truthfulness, and the worst of his misdoings were kept secret from the public. Perhaps his manners were not such as society, though very easy in those days, could tolerate; perhaps—but this is simple guesswork. All we know of Defoe is that as a writer he was of the greatest influence and note, but as a man nothing. He died poor and alone; he had little reward for unexampled labor. When Addison was secretary of state, and Prior an ambassador, he was nobody — a sword in the hand of an unscrupulous statesman; a shopkeeper manufacturing his genius and selling it by the yard. A sadder conclusion never was told.

CHAPTER V

ADDISON, THE HUMORIST

THERE is not a name in the entire range of English literature to which so full and universal an appreciation has been given by posterity as that of Addison. He had his critics in his day. He had, indeed, more than critics, and from one quarter at least has received in his breast the finest and sharpest sting which a friend estranged could put into poetic vengeance. But the burden even of contemporary voices was always overwhelmingly in his favor, and nowadays there is no one in the world, we believe, that has other than gentle words for the gentle writer—the finest critic, the finest gentleman, the most tender humorist of his age. It is not only admiration, but a sort of personal affection with which we look back, detecting in all the bustling companies of that witty and depraved period his genial figure, with a delightful simplicity in the midst of all the formalism, and whole-heartedness among the conceits and pretensions, of the fops and wits, the intriguing statesmen and busy conspirators, of an age in which public faith can scarcely be said to have existed at all. He had his little defects, which were the defects of the time. And perhaps his age would not have loved him as it did had he been entirely without a share in its weaknesses. As it was, no one could call him a milksop then, as no one would venture to record any offensive name against him now. The smile of benevolent good nature, of indulgent humor, of observation always as sweet and merci-

ful as it is acute and refined, is never absent from his countenance.   He treats no man hardly; the ideal beings whom he
creates are the friends of all: we could, indeed, more easily
spare dozens of living acquaintances than we could part with
Sir Roger de Coverley.   Addison is the very embodiment of
that delightful gift of humor on which we pride ourselves so
much as a specially English quality; his soft laugh touches all
the chords of sympathy and loving comprehension with a tender ridicule in which the applauses of admiration are conveyed
with double effect.   That his style is the perfection, in its way,
of English style is less dear and delightful to us than that what
it conveys is the perfection of feeling.   His art is the antipodes
of that satirical art which allows human excellence only to gird
at it, and insinuate motives which diminish or destroy.   Addison, on the other hand, allows imperfections which his interpretation turns into something more sweet than virtue, and throws
a delightful gleam of love and laughter upon the eccentricities
and characteristic follies of individual nature.   That he sees
everything is one of the conditions of his genial forgiveness of
everything that is not mean or base or cruel.   With these he
makes no terms.   They are not within the range of his treatment.   *Non ragionam di lor.*   He passes by to the genial rural
circle where all is honest, simple, and true; or to town, where in
the coffee-houses themselves a kind soul will find humors enough
to keep him cheerful without harm to any of his fellow-creatures—even the post-writers whom he jocularly recommends to
a supplementary Chelsea as having killed more men in the wars
than any general ever did, or the "needy persons" hungry for
news, whom he promises to keep supplied with good and wholesome sentiments.   He was at the same time the first of his
kind.   Thackeray associates Congreve—one does not exactly
know why—with this nobler name: but at once makes it clear
that there could be no comparison between them, since the world

of the comedy-writer was an entirely fictitious world, altogether
unlike the human nature of the essayist. Of the humorists we
may venture to say that Addison is the first, as well as the most
refined and complete. Swift draws a heavier shaft, which lacer-
ates and kills, and Pope sends his needle-pointed arrows, all
touched with poisonous venom, to the most vulnerable points;
but Addison has no heart to slay. He transfixes the veil of
folly with light, shining, irresistible darts, and pins it aloft in
triumph, but he lets the fool go free — perhaps lets you see even,
by some reflection from his swift-flying polished spear, a gleam
of human meaning in the poor wretch's face which touches
your heart. Even when he diverts himself with Tom Folio or
Ned Softly, instead of plunging these bores into a bottomless
gulf of contempt, he plays with them as one might with a child,
a twinkle of soft fun in his eye, drawing out their simple absurdities. That habit of his which Swift describes to Stella, as one
which she herself shared, of seeming to consent to follies which
it is not worth while contradicting, and which Pope venomously
characterizes as "assents with evil leer," lures him, and us
along with him, into byways of human nature which the impatient critic closes with a kick, and in which there is much amusement and little harm. Molière's *Trissotin* is a social conspira-
tor meaning to build advancement upon his bad verses; but
Addison's poetaster is only an exposition of harmless vanity,
humored by the gently malicious, but kind and patient, listener,
who amid his laughter finds a certain pleasure in pleasing the
victim too. There is sympathy even in the dissection, a conjunction of feelings which is of the very nature of the true humorist. These, no doubt, are of a very different caliber from that
creation which still charms the reader — the delightful figure of
Sir Roger, and all the simple folks full of follies and of virtues
who surround him; but they are scarcely less remarkable. The
lesser pictures, taken at a sitting in which the author has had

no time to elaborate those features of human character which always draw forth his tenderness, are yet full of this instinctive sweetness, as well as of insight, keen, though always tempered, as the touch of Ithuriel's spear. The angel, indeed, was far more severe, disclosing the demon under his innocent disguise; but Addison has nothing to do with demons, he has no deep-laid plan of mischief to unveil. The worst he does is to smile and banter the little absurdities out of us—those curious little delusions which deceive ourselves as well as the world.

This most loved of English writers was the son of one of those English parsons who confuse our belief in the extremely unfavorable account, given by both the graver and the lighter historians of the time, of the condition of country clergymen. Neither Parson Adams in his virtue, nor Parson Trulliber in his grossness, nor Macaulay's keen and clear picture, nor Thackeray's fine disrespectful studies of the chaplain who marries the waiting-maid, seem to afford us any guidance to the nature of the household which the Rev. Launcelot Addison, after many wanderings and experiences, set up in the little parish of Milston in Wiltshire somewhere about the year 1670. Steele's description of it has, no doubt, the artificial form affected by the age, and sets it forth as one of those models of perfection and examples to the world which nowadays we are more disposed to distrust and laugh at than to follow. "I remember among all my acquaintances," he says, "but one man whom I have thought to live with his children with equanimity and a good grace"; and he goes on to describe the "three sons and one daughter whom he bred with all the care imaginable in a liberal and ingenious way—their thoughts turned into an emulation for the superiority in kind and generous affection toward each other," the boys behaving themselves with a manly friendship, their sister treated by them with as much complaisance as any other young lady of their acquaintance. "It was an unspeakable pleasure to visit or sit at a meal in this family," he adds. " I have often seen the old man's heart flow at his eyes with joy upon occasions which would appear indifferent to such as were strangers to the turn of his mind; but a very slight accident wherein he saw his children's good will to one another created in him the Godlike pleasure of loving them because they loved one another." The family tenderness thus inculcated no doubt came from a mind full of the milk of human kindness, and happily transmitting that possession to the gentle soul of the eldest son, who probably was the one whom the father " had the weakness to love much better than the others "—a weakness which " he took as much pains to correct as any other criminal passion that could arise in his mind." Such a paternity and training does something to account for the prevailing gentleness of Addison's temper and judgments.

Dr. Addison had seen the world not in a very brilliant or luxurious way. He had been chaplain at Dunkirk, and afterward at Tangier among the Moors, upon which latter strange experience he wrote a book : and he rose afterward to be Dean of Lichfield, a dignified clergyman. One of the brothers went to India, and attained to some eminence ; the other was eventually, like Joseph, a fellow of Magdalen. They dispersed themselves in the world as the children of a clergyman might very well do at the present day, and it is evident belonged distinctly to the caste of gentlemen. The sons, or at least the son with whom we have specially to do, after sundry local schoolings went to Charterhouse, which he left at fifteen for Oxford, perhaps because of his unusual advancement, more probably because the custom of the time sent boys earlier to the university, as is still the practice in Scotland. Addison was much distinguished in that elegant branch of learning, the writing of Latin verse, a kind of distinction which remains dear to the finest minds, in spite of all the remarks concerning its inutility and the time wasted in acquiring the art, which the rest of the world has so largely indulged in. A copy of verses upon the accession of King William, written while he was still a very youthful scholar at Queen's College, no more than seventeen, got him his first promotion. The boy's verses came—perhaps from some proud tutor at Queen's, boasting what could be done under the cupola in the High street, finer than anything attempted in more distinguished seats of learning—into the hands of the Provost of Magdalen, to the amazement and envy of that more learned corporation. There had been no election of scholars in the previous year, during the melancholy time when the college was embroiled with King James, and the courtly Quaker Penn had all the disturbed and troubled fellows under his heel; but now that freedom had returned with the revolution and the heaven-sent William, there was room for a double number of distinguished poor demies. Dr. Lancaster of Magdalen decided at once that to leave such Latinity as that of the young author of these verses to a college never very great in such gifts would be a sin against his own: and young Addison was accordingly elected to all the privileges of a Magdalen demyship. It is with this beautiful college that his name is connected in Oxford. There could be no more fit association. The noble trees and velvet lawns of Magdalen speckled with deer, shy yet friendly creatures that embellish the retired and silent glades—the long-winding walk by the Cherwell round the meadows where the fritillaries grow, the time-worn dignity of the place with its graceful old-world architecture and associations, are all in the finest keeping with the shy and silent student who talked so little and thought so much, living among his books in his college rooms, keeping his lamp alight half through the night, or musing under the elms, where the little stream joins the greater. It is dreadful to think that in all probability Addison thought the imposing classicism of

Queen's, at which the cultivated scholar of to-day shudders, much finer than Magdalen: for he had no opinion of Gothic, and lamented the weakness if not wickedness, of those mistaken ages which wasted ornament upon such antiquated forms; but at least he loved his retired promenade under the trees, with all its sweetness of primrose and thrush in spring, and the wonderful yellow sunsets over the floods in winter, and the pleasant illusions of the winding way. There the stranger may realize still in the quiet of the cloistered shades how the shy young student wandered in Addison's Walk and pondered his verses, and formed the delicate wealth of speech which was to distinguish him from all his fellows. He spent about ten years in his college, first as a student and then as a fellow, in the position which, perhaps, is more ideal for a scholar than any other in Christendom. But the young man was not much more enlightened than the other young men of his age, notwithstanding his genius at Latin verses, and that still finer genius which had not as yet come to utterance. He wrote an "Account of the Greatest English Poets," not much wiser than the school-boy essays of our own day which set Lord Tennyson and Mr. Browning down in their right places. Addison went further. He leaves out all mention of Shakspere, and speaks of Cowley as a "mighty genius." He describes "the spacious times of great Elizabeth" as "a barbarous age," amused by "Old Spenser" with "long-spun allegories" and "dull morals," which have lost all power to charm an age of understanding. The youth, indeed, ran amuck among all the greatest names till we shiver at his temerity. But he knew better afterward; and, if he still condescended a little to his elders and betters, learned to love and comprehend them too.

It would seem that he wavered for a time whether he should not take orders, a step necessary to retain his fellowship, and dedicate himself to the church, as was the wish of his father.

It would have been entirely suitable to him one cannot but think; to his meditative mood, and shy temper, and high moral tone. He would have missed the humors of town, the coffee-houses, and the wits, and the vagaries of the beaus and belles; but with still a tenderer and more genial humor might have made his villagers live before us, and found out all the amusing follies of the knights and squires, which even in London town did not escape his smiling observation. The manner in which the question was decided is curiously characteristic of the age. That he was not himself inclined that way seems probable, since he bids his muse farewell after the fashion of the time, when this ending seemed imminent, with something like regret, and it is said that he distrusted his own fitness for the sacred office. At all events, the matter came to the ears of Charles Montague, afterward Lord Halifax, himself an elegant scholar, and at that time in office. Young Addison had addressed to him, on the occasion of the Peace of Ryswick in 1697, one of those pieces of Latin verse for which the young man was known among the scholars of his time. He accompanied the gift with a letter couched in the hyperbole of the age, deprecating his patron's possible disapproval of "the noble subject debased by my numbers," and justifying himself by the poverty of the verses already published on the same theme. "For my part," he says, "I never could prevail on myself to offer you a poem written in our native tongue, since you yourself deter all others by your own Compositions from such an Attempt, as much as you excite them by your Favour and Humanity." Montague returned this compliment by interfering in the young poet's concerns as soon as he heard of the danger that so promising a youth might fall into the gulf of the church, and be lost to the other kinds of work more useful to statesmen. He wrote to the authorities of Magdalen begging that Addison might not be urged into holy orders, and in the mean time took more active measures to secure him for the state. Lord Somers had also received the dedication of some of Addison's verses, and was equally interested in the young man's career. Between them the two statesmen secured for him a pension of three hundred a year, on no pretense of work to be done or duty fulfilled, but merely that he might be able to prepare himself the better for the public service, and be thus at hand and ready when his work was wanted. Public opinion has risen up nowadays against any such arrangement, and much slighter efforts at patronage would be denounced now over all England as a job. And yet one wonders whether it was so profitless a proceeding as we think it. Addison was worth more than the money to England. To be sure, without the money he would still have been Addison; yet something, no doubt, of the mellow sweetness of humanity in him was due to this fostering of his youth.

He went abroad in 1699, and addressed himself in the first place to the learning of French, which he did slowly at Blois, without apparently gaining much enlightenment as to the state of France or the other countries which he visited in his prolonged tour. No doubt, with his pension and the income of his fellowship, Addison traveled like a young man of fortune and fashion in those times of leisure, with excellent introductions everywhere, seeing the best society, and the greatest men both in rank and letters. Boileau admired his Latin verses as much as the English statesmen did, and the young man went upon his way more and more convinced that Latin verses were the highroad to fame. From France he went to Italy, making a classical pilgrimage. "Throughout," says Mr. Leslie Stephen, quaintly, "if we are to judge by his narrative, he seems to have considered the scenery as designed to illustrate his beloved poets." The much-debated uses of travel receive a new question from the records of such a journey, pursued with the fullest leisure and under the best auspices; and one wonders whether the man who hurries across a continent in a few weeks, catching flying impressions, and forming crude judgments, is, after all, much less advantaged than he who, oblivious of all the human interests around him, discusses Rome, for instance, as if it had no interest later than Martial or Silius Italicus—as if neither Church, nor Pope, nor all the convulsions of the Middle Ages, nor Crusader, nor Jesuit, had ever been.   This extraordinary impoverishment of the imagination was the fashion of the time, just as it has been the fashion in other days to fix upon the vile records of the Renaissance as the one thing interesting in the history of a noble country.   According to that fashion, however, Addison did everything that a young man of the highest culture could be expected to do.   He traced the footsteps of Æneas, and remembered every spot on which a classical battle had been fought, or an ode sung.   He wrote an eloquent essay upon medals, and lingered among the sculptures of the museums; and he picked up a subject for a heroic tragedy from the suggestion of a foolish play which he saw at a Venetian theater.   With his head full of such themes, he had gone out from Oxford, and with a deepened sense of their importance he came back again.   Though in after days he touches lightly with his satiric dart the young man who can talk of nothing better on his return than how "he had like to have been drowned at such a place; how he fell out of a chaise at another"; yet in the hymn of praise with which he celebrates his own return from all the dangers of foreign travel something like the same record is made, though in a more imposing manner:

> In foreign Realms and Lands remote,
>   Supported by thy care,
> Thro' burning Climes I passed unhurt,
>   And breath'd in Tainted Air.
> Thy mercy sweetened every Soil,
>   Made every Region please,
> The hoary Alpine Hills it warmed,
>   And smooth'd the Tyrrhene Seas.

JOSEPH ADDISON.

ENGRAVED BY T. JOHNSON, FROM MEZZOTINT BY JEAN SIMON,
AFTER PAINTING BY SIR GODFREY KNELLER.

It is only the vulgarity of our modern imagination that makes us think of hot water-pipes when the idea of warming the Alps is presented to our profane minds. The burrowing of the railway that climbs the St. Gothard may be taken as a large contribution to the carrying out of this suggestion.

When Addison returned home after these four years of classical wanderings, it was to prospects sadly overcast. King William had died a year before, which had stopped his pension; Halifax was out of office, and all the hopes of public life, for which he had been training himself, seemed to drop as he came back. It is said that during the last year he had charge of a pupil; but there is no proof of the statement, nor has any pupil ever been identified by name. An offer was made to him to accompany upon his travels a son of the Duke of Somerset, his services to be paid by the present of a hundred guineas at the year's end, which did not seem to Addison an advantageous offer: but this, which came to nothing, is the only authentic reference to any possible "bear-leading" such as Thackeray refers to in "Esmond"; and fine as is the sketch made by that kindred humorist, he seems to exaggerate at once the poverty and the neglect into which for the moment Addison fell.

He returned to England in 1703, being then thirty-one, full of every accomplishment, but with only his fellowship to depend upon, and the uncertain chances of Jacob Tonson's favor instead of the king's. He is said to have sunk, or rather risen, to a poor lodging in London, in the Haymarket, up three pairs of stairs, which was indeed a sad change from the importance of his position as a rich young Englishman making the grand tour. But if he carried a disappointed or despondent heart to those elevated quarters, he never made any moan on the subject, and it is very likely enjoyed his freedom and the happy sense of being at home like other young men; and he seems to have been at once advanced to the membership of the Kit-Cat Club, which would supply him with the finest of company, and a center for the life which otherwise must have appeared as if it had come to a broken end.   It was not long, however, that this period of neglect was suffered to last, and once more the transaction which elevated Addison to the sphere in which he passed the rest of his life is admirably characteristic of the period, and alas! profoundly unlike anything that could happen to a young man of genius now.

We will not return again to any bewildering discussion of the Whigs and Tories of Queen Anne, but only say that Godolphin and Marlborough, those "great twin brethren" of the state, had come into possession of England at this great crisis, and that every means by which they could secure the suffrages of both parties were doubly necessary, considering the disappointment on one side that the policy of the country remained unchanged, and on the other that it had to be carried out by Whig, not Tory, hands.   Nothing could be better adapted than the great victory of Blenheim to arouse an outburst of national feeling, and sweep, for a time at least, the punctilios of party away.   The lord treasurer, who had everything in his hands at home, while his great partner fought and conquered abroad, was almost comically at a loss how to sound the trumpet of warlike success so as to excite the country, and, if possible, turn the head of the discontented.   In one of Leopardi's fables there is an account of the tremendous catastrophe with which the world was threatened when his illustrious excellency the Sun declined one morning to rise and tread his old-world course around the earth for the comfort of mankind.   "Let her in her turn go round me if she wants my warmth and light," says the potentate—with great reason, it must be allowed, since Copernicus was born, and everything in the celestial spheres was about to be set right.   But how to persuade the earth that she must now undertake this circuit? Let a poet be found to do it is the first suggestion. "La via più spedita è la più sicura è di trovare un poeta ovvero un filosofo che persuada alla Terra di muoversi." Godolphin found himself in the same position as that in which the luckless agencies of the Universe were left when the Sun struck work. A poet!—but where to find a poet he knew not, being himself addicted to other modes of exercise and entertainment. He went to Halifax to ask where he should find what was wanted—a poet. But that statesman was coy and held back. He could, indeed, produce the very man; but why should he interfere to betray neglected merit and induce a man of genius to labor for those who would leave him to perish in obscurity? Godolphin, however, was ready to promise anything in the great necessity of the case; and Halifax permitted himself to be persuaded to mention the name which no doubt was bursting from his lips. He would not, however, undertake to be the ambassador, but insisted that the real possessors of power should ask in their own persons, and with immediate and substantial proofs of their readiness to recompense the service they demanded. That day, all blazing in gold lace and splendor, the coach of the chancellor of the exchequer stopped before the little shop in the Haymarket over which the young scholar had his airy abode: and that great personage clambered up the long flights of stairs carrying with him, very possibly, the patent of the appointment which was an earnest of what the powers that were could do for Addison. This was how the great poem of the "Campaign," that illustrious composition, was brought into being. Poems made to order seldom fulfil expectation, but in this case there was no disappointment. Godolphin and England alike were delighted, and Addison's life and success were at once secured

No one now save as an illustration of history, would think

of reading the "Campaign," though most readers are familiar
with the famous simile which dazzled a whole generation:

> 'T was there great Marlborough's mighty soul was proved,
> That in the shock of charging hosts unmoved,
> Amidst confusion, horror, and despair
> Examined all the dreadful scenes of war,
> In powerful thought the field of death surveyed,
> To fainting squadrons sent the timely aid,
> Inspired repulsed battalions to engage,
> And taught the doubtful battle where to rage.
> So when an angel by Divine command
> With rising tempest shakes a guilty land,
> Such as of late o'er pale Britannia past,
> Calm and serene he drives the furious blast;
> And, pleased the Almighty's orders to perform,
> Rides in the whirlwind, and directs the storm.

Macaulay points out with much felicity how the fact of the
Great Storm—so called in English history—which had passed
over England in the previous year, and was yet full in the memory of all, gave strength and meaning to this famous simile,
which at once opened to Addison the gates of fortune and of
fame.   Two years after he was promoted to be one of the under-
secretaries of state, and from that time languished no more in
the cold shade of obscurity where Halifax had upbraided the
Government for leaving him.   He was not a man born to linger
there.   Shy though he was, and little apt to put himself forward, this favorite of the muses—to use the phraseology of his
time—was also the favorite of fortune.   Everything that he
touched throve with him.   The gifts he possessed were all
especially adapted to the requirements of his time.   At no
other period, perhaps, in history did the rulers of the country bethink themselves of a poet as the auxiliary most necessary: and his age was the only one that relished poetry of
Addison's kind.

This event brought more than mere prosperity to the fortunate young man. If he had been already of note enough to
belong to the Kit-Cat Club, with what a blaze of modest glory
would he now appear—not swelling in self-conceit, like so many
of the wits; not full of silent passion, like the strange big Irish
clergyman who pushed into the chattering company in the coffee-house and astounded them with his masterful and arrogant
ways: but always modest—never heard at all in a large company, opening out a little when the group dispersed, and an audience fit but few gathered around him—but with one companion
half divine. The one companion by and by became often that
very same Irishman whose silent prowl about the room in which
he knew nobody had amused all the luckier members. Swift
found himself in a kind of coffee-house paradise when he got
Addison alone, and the two took their wine together, spending
their half-crowns according to the stranger's thrifty record, and
wishing for no third. They were as unlike as could be conceived in every particular and yet what company they must
have been, as they sat together, the wine going a little too
freely—though Swift was always temperate, and Addison, notwithstanding that common peccadillo, the most irreproachable
of men! It was then that the "Travels in Italy" were published, while still the fame of the "Campaign" was warm; and
Addison gave his new friend a copy inscribed to "Jonathan
Swift, the most Agreeable Companion, the Truest Friend, and the
Greatest Genius of his Age." What quick understanding, what
recognition as of two who had been born to know each other!
They were both in their prime—Swift thirty-eight, Addison
five years younger, still young enough to hope for everything
that can befall a man; the one fully entered upon the path of
fortune, the other surely so much nearer it for being thus received and welcomed. Addison gave "his little senate laws"
for many years in these convivial meetings, and all who sur-

12*

rounded him adored him.   But Swift was never again so close a
member of the little company.   Politics, and the curious part
which the Irish parson took in them, separated him from the
consistent and moderate politician, who acted faithfully with his
party, and who was always true whoever might be false.   But
Swift held fast to Addison so far at least as feeling was concerned.   Over and over he repeated the sentiment, that " if he
had a mind to be king he would hardly be refused."   Their
meetings ceased, and all those outflowings of wit and wisdom,
and the talk long into the night which was the most delightful
thing in life ; but for years after Swift still continued to say that
there was nothing his friend might not be if he would : that his
election was carried without a word of opposition when every
other member had to fight for his life, and that he might be king
in Ireland, or anywhere else, had he the mind.   They were used
to terms of large applause in those days, but to no one else did
it take this particular form.

In 1708 Addison lost his post as under-secretary by a change
of the ministry, or rather of the minister, it being the habit in
those days to form a government piecemeal, a Whig here, a
Tory there, as favor or circumstances required, so that it was by
no means needful that all should go out or come in together.
In fact, no sooner was the under-secretary deprived of one place
than he obtained another, that of secretary to the lord lieuten-
ant of Ireland, the same office, we presume, as that which is
now called chief secretary for Ireland, though its seriousness
and power are now so much greater.   In those days there was
no Irish people to deal with, but only a very lively, contentious,
pushing, and place-hunting community—the Protestant English-Irish, which, so far as literature and public knowledge go,
has been accepted as the type of the much darker and less simple character of the Celt.   The wild, mystic, morose, and often
cruel nature of the native race, with its gleams of poetry and

dreams of fortune, has turned out a very different thing to reckon with. No such problem was presented to the statesmen of that time. The admixture of Irish blood would seem to go to the head of the Saxon and endow him with a gaiety and sparkle which does not exist either in one race or the other unmixed; and it was with the society formed on this basis, the ascendant minority, contemptuous of every possible power of the people so-called, yet far less unsympathetic than the anxious politicians of to-day, that Addison had to deal. His post was "very lucrative," we are told—in fees and pieces of patronage, no doubt, for the income was but £2000 a year —and he soon acquired an even greater popularity on the one side of the channel than on the other. Something amiable and conciliatory must have rayed out of the man : otherwise it is curious to understand the popularity in brilliant and talkative Dublin of a stranger whose chief efforts in conversation were only to be accomplished *tête-à-tête*. But he had the foil of a detestable and detested chief—Wharton, whose corrupt and brutal character gave double acceptance to the secretary's charm and goodness, and the Tories contended with the Whigs, says Swift, which should speak best of this favorite of fortune. "How can you think so meanly of a kingdom," he exclaims, "as not to be pleased that every creature in it who hath one grain of worth has a veneration for you?" It is not often that even in hyperbole such a thing can be said.

It was while Addison was in Ireland thus gathering golden opinions that an event occurred which was of the utmost importance to his reputation, so far especially as posterity was concerned. Among the little band of friends over whom he held a kind of genial sway, and who acknowledged his superiority with boundless devotion, was one who was more nearly his equal than any other of the band ; a friend of youth, one of those erratic but generous natures whose love of excellence is almost rapturous, though they are unable themselves to keep up to the high level they approve. Steele can never be forgotten where Addison is honored. He had been at Charterhouse and at Oxford along with his friend, and no doubt it was a wonder among the reading men in their earlier days how it was that the correct, the polished, the irreproachable scholar of Magdalen, with his quiet ways, could put up with that gay scapegrace who was perpetually in trouble. Such alliances, however, have not been rare. The cheerful, careless Dick, full of expedients, full of animal spirits, always amusing, friendly, generous in his impulses, if unintentionally selfish in the constant breaches of his better meaning, must have had a charm for the steadier and purer nature which was formed with pulses more orderly. No doubt Steele's perpetual self-revelation, his unfolding of a hundred quips and cranks of human nature, and unsuspicious rendering up of all his natural anomalies and contradictions to the instinctive spectatorship of his amused companion, helped to endear him to the humorist, who must have laughed till he cried on many an occasion over poor Dick's amazing wisdoms and follies, without any breach of that indulgent affection which between two men who have grown up together can rarely be said to be mingled with anything so keen as contempt. Steele, it is evident, must have known Addison "at home," as school-boys say, or he could not have made that little sketch of the household where brothers and sisters were taught to be so loving to each other. While the young hero who had, as in the favorite allegories of the time, chosen the right path, and taken the steady hand of Minerva, instead of that more lovely one of fatal Venus to guide him, was reaching the heights of applause and good fortune, the unlucky youth who chose pleasure for his pursuit had gone disastrously the other way, and fallen into all sorts of adventures, extremely amusing for his friend to hear of, though he disapproved, and no doubt very amusing to the actual actor in them, though he suffered. But Addison was not a mere "spectator" so far as the friend of his youth was concerned. When he began to rise there seems little reason to doubt that he pulled Steele up with him, introducing him to the notice of the fine people, who in those days might make the fortune of a gentlemanly and clever adventurer, and that either by his own interest or that of one of his powerful friends he procured him a place and started him in public life. Steele had already floated into literature, and, whether it is true or not that Addison helped him in the concoction of one play at least, it is clear that he kept his purse and his heart well open to his friend, now a man about town ruffling at the coffee-houses with the best, and full of that energy and readiness which so often strike out new ways of working, though it may require steadier heads to carry them out.

It was, however, while Addison was in Ireland that Steele was moved by the most important of these original impulses, an idea full, as it proved, of merit and practical use. Journalism was then in its infancy. A little "News Letter," or "Flying Post"—a shabby broadsheet containing the bulletin of a battle, a formal and brief notice of parliamentary proceedings, an account of some monstrous birth, a child with two heads, or that perennial gooseberry which has survived into our own time—and an elaborate list of births, deaths, and marriages, was almost all that existed in the way of public record. The post to which Steele had been appointed was that of Gazetteer, which naturally led him to the consideration of such matters: and among the crowd of projects which worked together in his "barmy noddle," there suddenly surged uppermost the idea of a paper which should come out on the post days, the Tuesdays, Thursdays, and Saturdays which were, up to that time, the only days of communication with the country; a paper written after the fancy of the time, in itself a letter from the

wits and the knowing persons in town, revealing not only the
existing state of public affairs, but all those exquisite particulars
of society which have always been the delight of country cir-
cles, and which were doubly sure to please at a time when society was governed by talk, when all public criticism was verbal,
and the echoes of the wits in the coffee-houses were blown
about on all the breezes.   Happy the Sir Harry who, sitting
mum over his wine in a corner, could hear these gentlemen discussing what Sunderland or Somers had said, what my Lord
Treasurer intended, or, more delightful, the newest incident in
the tragedy-comedy of the great duchess — how the queen
looked glumly at her over the card-table, or let her stand unno-
ticed at a drawing-room ; and still more deeply blest the parson who had Mr. Addison pointed out to him, and heard the
young Templars and scholars pressing him with questions as to
when his " Cato " was coming out, or asking his opinion on a
set of verses.   Such worthies would go back to the country
full of these reflections from the world, and tell how the gallants
laughed at the mantua which was going out of fashion, and
made fun of the red heels which, perhaps, were just then ap-
pearing at the Manor or the Moated Grange.   Steele saw at
once what a thing it would be to convey these impressions at
first hand in a privileged " Tatler " direct to the houses of the
gentry all over the country.   Perhaps he did not perceive at
first what a still finer thing to have them served up with the
foaming chocolate or fragrant tea at every breakfast in Mayfair.

It is an idea that has occurred to a great many heads since
with less success.   In these latter days there have been many
literary adventurers, to whom the starting of a new paper has
seemed an opening into El Dorado.   But the opening in the
majority of cases does not prove a practicable one — for, in
fact, there is no longer any need of news ; and the concise little
essays and elegant banterings of those critics of the time have

fallen out of date. News means in our day an elaborate system, and instantaneous reports from all the world; and one London newspaper—far more one of the gigantic journals proper to America—contains as much matter as half a hundred "Tatlers." One wonders, if Addison's genius, and the light hand of Steele, and Swift's tremendous and scathing humor could be conjured up again, whether such a production, with its mingled thread of the finest sentiments and the pettiest subjects, metaphysics and morals, and the "Eneid" and "Paradise Lost," and periwigs and petticoats, would find sufficient acceptance with "the fair" and the wise to keep it afloat, or would still go up to sages and fine ladies with their breakfast trays.

It was on the immediate foundation of one of Swift's savage *jeux d'esprits* that the new undertaking was begun, a mystification which greatly amused the wits then, but which does not, perhaps, appear particularly delightful now. Swift had been seized by a freak of mischief in respect to a certain Partridge, an astrologer, who made an income out of the public by pretended revelations of the future, as is still done, we believe, among those masses, beneath the ascertained audience of literature, who spend their sixpences at Christmas upon almanacs and year-books containing predictions of what is to happen. It occurred to Swift in some merry moment to emulate and to doom the Merlin of the day: and with the prodigious gravity which characterizes his greatest jests he wrote "Predictions for the year 1708," in which, among many other things, he announced that he had consulted the stars on behalf of Partridge, and had ascertained that the wizard would certainly die on March 29, at eleven o'clock at night, of a raging fever. The reader will probably remember that the jest was kept up, and that, notwithstanding Partridge's protest that he was not dead at all, Isaac Bickerstaff insisted on asserting that his prophecy had been fulfilled, to the grave confusion of various serious affairs, and the inextinguishable laughter of the wits. It was not a pretty jest, but it brought into being a visionary critic of public matters, a new personage in the literary world, in whom other wits saw capabilities. Steele in particular perceived that Isaac Bickerstaff was just the personality he wanted, and therewith proceeded to make of that shadowy being the Mentor of the time. The design was excellent, the immediate execution cleverly adapted to seize the interest of the public, which had been already amused and mystified under that name. Mr. Isaac Bickerstaff presented his readers with the first number of his journal without charge. " I earnestly desire," he says, " all persons, without distinction, to take it in for the present *gratis*, and hereafter at the price of one penny, forbidding all hawkers to take more for it at their peril." The idea took the town. No doubt there would be many an allusion to this and that which the wits would guess at, and which would to them have a double meaning ; but, to do the " Tatler " justice, the kind of gossip which fills the so-called society newspapers in our day was unknown to the witty gentlemen who sometimes satirize a ruffle or a shoe-tie, but never personally a woman. The types of fine ladies who flutter through his pages could never raise a pang in any individual bosom ; and when he addressed himself to the reform of the theater, to the difficult duty of checking play and discouraging duels, he had all the well-thinking on his side.

Steele had gone on for some numbers before his new venture attracted the attention of Addison. He recognized whose the hand was from a classical criticism in the sixth number which he had himself made to Steele ; and he must have been pleased with the idea, since he soon after appears as a coadjutor, sending his contributions from the Secretary's office in Dublin. There has been a great and prolonged controversy upon the respective merits of these two friends : some, and

first among them Macaulay will have it that Addison had all
the merit of the publication. "Almost everything good in the
'Tatler' was his," says the historian. But there are many
who, despite Macaulay's great authority, find a certain difficulty in distinguishing Addison from Steele and Steele from
Addison, and are inclined to find the latter writer as entertaining and as gifted as the former. No question could be more
difficult to settle. As we glance over the little gray volumes
which bring back to us dimly the effect which the little broadsheet must have had when it appeared day by day, there is no
doubt that the eye is oftenest caught by something which,
when we look again, proves to be from Addison's hand. We
open, it is by chance, and yet not altogether by chance, upon
Tom Folio and his humors; upon the poor poet and his
verses; upon some group of shabby heroes, or stumbling procession of country gentlemen which there is no mistaking. But
on the other hand it is Steele who gives us that family picture,
which reads like the Vicar of Wakefield, yet with a more
tender touch (for Mrs. Primrose was never her husband's
equal), showing us the good woman among her family, the
husband half distracted with the fear of losing her, the wife for
his sake smiling her paleness away. Indeed, we think, in these
early essays at least, it would be a mistake for the critic to risk
his reputation on the superiority of Addison. He set up no
higher standard than that which his friend had raised, but fell
into the same humor, adding his contribution of social pictures
with less force of moral generally, and more delicacy of work-
manship, but no remarkable preëminence. The character of
the publication changed gradually as the great new pen came
into it; but whether by Addison's influence or by the mere action of time, and a sense of what suited the audience he had
obtained — which a soul so sympathetic as Steele's would
naturally divine with readiness — no one can tell. Gradually

the news which at first had regularly filled a column dropped away. It had been, no doubt, well authenticated news, the freshest and best, as it came from the authorized hand of the Gazetteer; but either Steele got tired of supplying it, or a sense of the inexpediency of publishing anything which might displease his patrons and the government, convinced him that it was unnecessary. It is scarcely possible, either, to tell why the "Tatler" came to an end. Mr. Austin Dobson, in his recent life of Steele, gives sundry reasons which do not seem, however, of any particular weight. Steele's own account is that he had become known, and his warnings and lessons were thus made of no avail:

I considered [he says] that severity of manners was absolutely necessary to him who would censure others, and for that reason and that only chose to talk in a mask. I shall not carry my humility so far as to call myself a vicious man, but at the same time confess my life is at best but pardonable. And with no greater character than this a man could make an indifferent progress in attacking prevailing and fashionable vices, which Mr. Bickerstaff has done with a freedom of spirit that would have lost both its beauty and efficacy had it been pretended to by Mr. Steele.

This reason is, however,— though pretty and just enough had its writer renounced the trade,— a somewhat fantastic one when we reflect that though the "Tatler" ended in January, 1711, the "Spectator" began in March of the same year. The one died only to be replaced by the other. It is said that Addison did not know of his friend's intention to cut the "Tatler" short, and it was he who was the chief agent in beginning the "Spectator." Therefore it may have been that the breach was but an impatience of Steele's, which his slow and less impulsive and more constant comrade could not permanently consent to. No doubt Addison had by this time learned the advantage of such a mode of utterance, and felt how entirely it suited his own manner of work and constitution of mind. The fictitious person of Isaac Bickerstaff was relinquished in the new series: it no longer assumed to give any news. Its contents were less varied, consisting generally of a single essay, and, notwithstanding the impression which the casual reader often has, and which some critics have largely dwelt upon, that the comments of this critic are upon the merest vanities of the time, the hoops, the gold-lace, the snuff-boxes, and patches of the period, it is astonishing how little space is actually taken up with these lighter details, and how many graver questions, how many fine sentiments and delicate situations, afford the moralist occasion for those remarks which he makes in the most beautiful and picturesque English to the edification of all the generations. There is, perhaps, no book which is so characteristic of an epoch in history, and none which gives so clear a conception of the English world of the time. We sit and look on, always amused, often instructed, while the delicate panorama unfolds before us—and see everything pass, the fine coaches, the gentlemen on foot, the parsons in their gowns, the young Templars jesting in the doorways: but always with the little monologue going on, which accompanies the movement, and runs off into a hundred byways of thought, sometimes serious, sometimes gay, often with no particular connection with the many-colored streams of passers-by, yet never obscuring our sight of them as they come and go. There is, perhaps, a noisy group at the door while Mr. Spectator talks, with their wigs in the last fashion, and their clouded canes hung to a button, while they discourse. In one corner there are some two or three grave gentlemen putting their heads together over the latest news; and in another the young fellows over their wine eager in discussion of Mrs. Oldfeld and Mrs. Bracegirdle at the theater, or of Chloe and Clarissa, the reigning beauties of society; or perhaps it is a poet, poor Ned Softly, as the case may be, who is reading his last sonnet to his mistress's eyebrow, amid the

laughing commentaries or the ridicule of his companions.
What is Mr. Spectator talking of all the while? His discourse
does not prevent us hearing the impertinences of the others.
Perhaps he is talking of honest love, a favorite theme of his,
at which the wits do not dare to laugh in his presence,— or he
is telling one of his fables, to which everybody in the midst of
his levity or his business gives half an ear at least; or by a
caprice he has turned aside to metaphysics, and is discussing the processes of the mind, and how "no thought can be
beautiful that is not just"; how "'t is a property of the heart of
man to be diffusive, its kind wishes spread abroad over the face
of the creation," and such like; not to speak of graver subjects
still to which he will direct our minds on Saturdays, perhaps to
prepare us for Sunday, when he is silent. Or he will read
aloud a letter from some whimsical correspondent, which the
wits will pause to hear, for gossip is ever sweet, but which before they know lands them in a case of hardship or trouble
which touches their consciences and rouses their pity. Sometimes the hum of life will stop altogether and even Softly put
his verses in his pocket to listen: and on the brink of tears the
fine gentlemen, and we too along with them, incontinently burst
out a-laughing at some touch that no one expected. But whether
we laugh or cry, or are shamed in our levity, or diverted in our
seriousness, outside the windows the crowd is always streaming
on. There is no separating the "Spectator" from the lively,
crowded, troublous, and perplexing scenes upon which all his
reflections are made. The young lady looking out of her
coach — at sight of whom all the young fellows doff their hats
and make their comments, how much her fortune is, who is in
pursuit of her, or if any mud has yet been flung upon her —
shows to the philosopher a face disturbed with all the puzzles
of an existence which nobody will allow her to take seriously.
The poor wit who endeavors so wistfully to amuse my lord in

SIDNEY, EARL OF GODOLPHIN.

ENGRAVED BY PETER AIKEN, FROM MEZZOTINT BY JOHN SMITH, IN BRITISH MUSEUM.
PAINTED BY SIR GODFREY KNELLER.

his dullness betrays to that critic not so much the soul of a
toady, as that of the anxious father with children that starve at
home. His young fellows, though they look so careless, have
their troubles too. Wherever that keen eye turns another
group shows through the crowd, or a lonely whimsical figure
as distinct as if there was no one but he. Save perhaps on
those Saturdays when he plays his soft accompaniment to Milton's grand, sonorous organ he is never abstracted or retired
from men: on all other occasions, though he is thinking of a
great deal else, and has his mind absorbed in other themes,
this busy world of which he forms a part is always with him.
Sometimes he permits us to see him over their heads only,
seated on his familiar bench at his table, from whence he de-
livers his homilies, with all these figures moving and re-mov-
ing on the busy pavement in the foreground; sometimes we
are admitted inside, and watch them through open door and
window by his side: but he is never to be parted from the
society in which he finds his models, his subjects, his audience.
Like other men he takes it for granted that the fashion of his
contemporaries is to go on forever. For posterity that smiling,
keen observer takes no thought.

But of all things else that Addison has done there remains
one preëminent figure which is his chief claim to immortality.
The " Campaign " has disappeared out of literature ; " Cato " is
known only by a few well-known lines; the " Spectator " itself,
though a work which no gentleman's library can be without, dwells
generally in dignified retirement there, and is seldom seen on
any table but the student's, though we are all supposed to be
familiar with it : but Sir Roger de Coverley is the familiar friend
of most people who have read anything at all, and the acquaintance by sight, if we may so speak, of everybody. There is no
form better known in all literature. His simple rustic state, his
modest sense of his own importance, his kind and genial patron-

age of the younger world, which would laugh at him if it were not overawed by his modesty and goodness, and which still sniggers in its sleeve at all those kind, ridiculous ways of his as he walks about in London, taken in on all sides, with his hand always in his purse and his heart in its right place, are always familiar and delightful.   We learn with a kind of shock that it was Steele who first introduced this perfect gentleman to the world, and can only hope that it was Addison's idea from the first, and that he did not merely snatch out of his friend's hands and appropriate a conception so entirely according to his own heart.   To Steele, too, we are indebted for some pretty scenes in the brief history : for Will the Huntsman's wooing, which is the most delicate little enamel, and for the knight's own love-making, which, however, is pushed a little too near absurdity. But it is Addison who leads him forth among his country neigh-bors, and to the assizes, and meets the gipsies with him, and brings him up to town, carrying him to Westminster and to Spring Gardens, in the wherry with the one-legged waterman, and to the play.   The delightful gentleman is never finer than in this latter scene.   He has to be conveyed in his coach, at-tended by all his servants, armed with "good oaken plants," and Captain Sentry in the sword he had worn at Steinkirk, for fear of the Mohocks, those brutal disturbers of the public peace whom Addison justly feels it would be unbecoming to bring within sight of his noble old knight.

As soon as the house was full and the candles lighted my old friend stood up and looked about him with that pleasure which a mind seasoned with humanity naturally feels in itself at the sight of a multi-tude of people who seem pleased with one another, and partake of the same common entertainment.   I could not but fancy to myself as the old man stood up in the middle of the pit that he made a very proper centre to a tragick Audience.   Upon the entering of Pyrrhus the Knight told me that he did not believe the King of France had a better strut. I was indeed very attentive to my old friend's remarks because I looked upon them as a piece of natural criticism and was well pleased to hear him, at the conclusion of almost every scene, telling me that he could not imagine how the play would end; one while he appeared much concerned for Andromache, and a little while after as much for Hermione; and was extremely puzzled to know what would become of Pyrrhus. When Sir Roger saw Andromache's obstinate refusal to her lover's importunities, he whispered me in the ear that he was sure she would never have him ; to which he added with a more than ordinary vehemence, " You can't imagine, sir, what 't is to have to do with a widow." Upon Pyrrhus, his threatening afterwards to leave her, the Knight shook his head and murmured, " Ay ! do it if you can." This part dwelt so much upon my friend's imagination that at the close of the third act, as I was thinking of something else, he whispered in my ear, " These widows, sir, are the most perverse creatures in the world. But pray," says he, " you that are a critick, is this play according to your dramatick rules, as you call them ? Should your People in Tragedy always talk to be understood ? Why, there is not a single sentence in this play that I do not know the meaning of ! "

The fourth act very luckily began before I had time to give the old gentleman an answer. " Well," says the Knight, sitting down with great satisfaction, " I suppose we are now to see Hector's Ghost ? " He then renewed his attention, and from time to time fell a-praising the widow. He made, indeed, a little mistake as to one of her pages, whom, at his first entering, he took for Astyanax ; but we quickly set him right in that particular, though at the same time he owned he should have been very glad to see the little boy, who, says he, must needs be a very fine child by the account that is given of him.

Could anything be more delightful than this genial picture? We have all met in later years a certain Colonel Newcome, who is very like Sir Roger, one of his descendants, though he died a bachelor. But the Worcestershire knight was the first of his lineage, and few are the gifted hands who have succeeded in framing men after his model. Those little follies which are so dear to us, the good faith which makes the young men laugh, yet feel ashamed of themselves for laughing, and all the circumstances of that stately simple life which are so different from anything we know, yet so lifelike and genuine, have grown into the imagination of the after-generations. We seem to know Sir Roger from our cradle, though we may never even have read the few chapters of his history. This is the one infallible distinction of genius above all commoner endowments. Of all the actors in that stirring time Sir Roger remains the most living and real. The queen and her court are no more than shadows moving across the historic stage. Halifax, and Somers, and Harley, and even the great Bolingbroke, what are they to us? Figures confused and uncertain, that appear and disappear in one combination or another, so that our head aches in the effort to follow, to identify, to make sure what the intrigues and the complications mean. But we have no difficulty in recollecting all about Sir Roger. We would not have the old man mocked at any more than Mr. Addison would, but kiss his kind old hand as we smile at those little foibles which are all ingratiating and delightful. In that generation, with all its wars and successes, there was, perhaps, no such gain as Sir Roger. Marlborough's victories made England feared and respected, but cost the country countless treasure, and gave her little advantage ; the good knight cost nobody anything, and made all the world the richer. He is one of those inhabitants who never grow old or pass away, and he gives us proof undeniable that when we speak of a corrupt and depraved age, as we have reason to do, we have still nobler reason for believing—as the despairing prophet was taught by God himself in far older times: that however dark might be the prospect there were still seven thousand men in Israel who had never bowed the knee to Baal—what we learn over again, thank Heaven! from shining example everywhere, that there are always surviving the seed of the just, the salt of the earth, by whose silent agency, and pure love, and honest truth, life is made practicable and the world rolls on.

Sir Roger is the great point of the " Spectator," as the " Spectator " is the truest history of the time. It contains,

however, beside, much that is admirable and entertaining, as
well as a good deal that was temporary, and is now beyond the
fashion of our understanding, or, at least, of our appreciation.
Addison's criticism, or rather exposition, of Milton, which no
doubt taught his age a far more general regard for that great
poet, is well enough known, but yet not nearly so well known
as Sir Roger, and not necessary now as it was then.   When
these criticisms began it is evident that Addison, as well as his
friend Steele, had made a great advance from the time when the
young Oxford scholar left Shakspere out of his reckoning altogether, and considered "Old Spenser" only fit to amuse a barbarous age.   Though the balance of things had not been re-
dressed throughout the English world, yet these scholars had
come to perceive that the greatness of their predecessors had
been, perhaps, a little mixed up ; that Cowley was not so mighty
a genius as their boyhood believed, and that there were figures
as of gods behind which it was shame to have misconceived.
Throughout all, the meaning was wholesome, and tended toward
the elevation of the time.   Steele had it specially at heart to
discourage gambling, and to put down the hateful tyranny of the
duel.   And both writers used all their powers to improve and
raise the character of theatrical representations, keeping a watch
not only over the plays that were performed, but also over the
manners of the audience, who crowded the stage so that the
players could scarcely be seen, and played cards in their boxes,
and used the public entertainment for their own private quarrels
and assignations.   It is curious, too, to note how these authorities regarded the opera, the new form of amusement which had
pushed its way, against all the prejudices of the English, into
fashion.   Addison himself, indeed, wrote an opera which was
not successful ; but he did not love that new-fangled entertainment.   He devotes two or three numbers to the description of
it, for, says he, "There is no question our grandchildren will be

13*

very anxious to know the reason why their forefathers used to
sit together like an audience of foreigners in their own country,
and to hear whole plays acted before them in a tongue which
they did not understand." It is evident by this that his age had
not reached to the further sublimity of believing that when the
utterance is musical there is no need of understanding at all.
"One scarce knows how to be serious," he adds, "in the con-
futation of an absurdity that shows itself at the first sight. It
does not want any great measure of sense to see the ridicule of
this monstrous practice. If the Italians have a genius for music
above the English, the English have a genius for other performances of a much higher nature, and capable of giving the
mind a much nobler entertainment." We wonder if our " Spectator " would be less affronted now by the constant adaptation
of equivocal French plays to the English stage, than by the
anomaly of a representation given in language which nobody
understood? He would, perhaps, feel it to be an advantage
often not to understand, and doubt whether the English after
all "have a genius for other performances of a much higher
nature."

We are not informed that the "Tatler" and "Spectator,"
the real foundation of his fame, gave Addison any help in his
career. That was assured by the "Campaign." He received
his first post, that of "a commissionership with £200 a year,"
at once, in the end of 1704: his pension having ceased at
King William's death in 1702: the interval is not a very long
one, and during this time he had retained his college fellowship. In 1706 he became under-secretary. In 1708, his chief,
Lord Sunderland, was dismissed, and Addison along with him;
but the latter stepped immediately into the Irish secretaryship,
which was worth £2000 a year. Two years afterward occurred
the political convulsions brought about by the trial of Sacheverell and the intrigues of the back stairs, which brought Harley

into power, and Addison with his leaders was once more out
of office; but in 1714 they came triumphantly back, and he rose
to the height of political elevation as secretary of state with a
seat in the Cabinet. Though he did not retain this position
long on account of his failing health, he retired on a pension of
£1500 a year. In 1711, at a period when he was supposed to
be at a low ebb of fortune, in the cold shade of political opposition, he was able to buy the estate of Bilton, near Rugby, for
which he paid £10,000 — which is not bad for a moment of misfortune. Altogether Addison was provided for as the deserving and honorable hero — the wise youth of one of his own
allegories, the good apprentice — should be, by poetic justice,
but is not always in the experience of the world. The success
of the " Spectator," however, which was more his than Steele's
(as the "Tatler" had been much more Steele's than Addison's),
was apparently very considerable ; Addison himself says, in an
early number, that it had reached the circulation of three thousand copies a day. On a special occasion fourteen thousand
copies are spoken of; and the passing of the Stamp Act, which
destroyed many of the weaker publications of the time, did comparatively little harm to the " Spectator," which doubled its price
without much diminishing its popularity. It had also what no
other daily, and very few periodicals of any time, ever reach, the
advantage of a permanent issue afterward, in a succession of
volumes, of which the first edition seems to have reached an
issue of ten thousand copies. Fortunate writers ! pleasant
public ! The "Times," and the rest of our great newspapers,
boast a circulation beyond that which the eighteenth century
could have dreamed of; and thirty years ago it was the fashion
among public orators more indebted to genius than education — Mr. Cobden for one, and, we think, Mr. John Bright —
to say that the leading articles of that day were more than equal
to Thucydides and all the other writers of whom classical

scholars made their boast. But we wonder how the "Times" leaders would read collected into a volume, against those little dingy books (tobacco paper, as a contemporary says) with all their wisdom and their wit. "I will not meddle with the 'Spectator,'" says Swift to Stella, "let him *fair sex* it to the world's end." And so he has, at least so far as the world has yet advanced toward that undesirable conclusion.

The "Spectator" ended with the year 1712, having existed less than two years. Whether the authors had found their audience beginning to fail, or their inspiration, or had considered it wise (as is most likely) to forestall the possibility of either catastrophe, we are not informed. Almost immediately after the conclusion of this greatest undertaking of his life, Addison plunged into what probably appeared to the weakness of contemporary vision a much greater undertaking, the production of his tragedy "Cato," which made a commotion in town such as few plays did even at that period. It was partly as a political movement, to stir up the patriotism and love of liberty which were supposed to be failing under the dominion of the Tories, suspected of all manner of evil designs, that his Whig friends urged Addison to bring out the great play which had been simmering in his brain since his travels, and which had no doubt been read in detached acts and pieces of declamation to all his literary friends. These friends had received several additions in the mean time, especially in the person of Pope, who was still young enough to be proud of Addison's notice, yet remarkable enough to be intrusted with the composition of a prologue to the great man's work. Swift, notwithstanding the coldness which had ensued between them on his change of politics, was still sufficiently in Addison's friendship to be present at a rehearsal, and the whole town on both sides was moved with excitement and expectation. On the first night, "our house," says Cibber, "was in a manner invested and entrance

demanded by twelve o'clock at noon ; and before one it was not
wide enough for many who came too late for their places." The
following account of its reception is given in a letter by Pope :

> The numerous and violent claps of the Whig party on the one side
> of the theatre were echoed back by the Tories on the other ; while the
> author sweated behind the scenes with concern to find their applause
> proceeding more from the hand than the head. This was the case, too,
> with the Prologue-writer, who was clapped into a sound Whig at the
> end of every two lines. I believe you have heard that, after all the
> applause of the opposite faction, my lord Bolingbroke sent for Booth,
> who played *Cato*, into the box between one of the acts, and presented
> him with fifty guineas, in acknowledgment, as he expressed it, for de-
> fending the cause of liberty so well against a perpetual dictator. The
> Whigs are unwilling to be distanced this way, and therefore design a
> present to the same *Cato* very speedily.

Bolingbroke's speech about a perpetual dictator was a gibe
which everybody understood, directed against the devotion of
the Whigs to Marlborough, and was quite honest warfare ; but
what, we wonder, would Mr. Irving think if Mr. Gladstone sent
for him to his box, and ' presented him with fifty guineas " ?
The actor who considers himself one of the most distinguished
members of good society had not been thought of in those days.
One wonders, too, in passing, where a fine gentleman kept his
money, and whether the purse of the stage, which is always
ready to be flung to a deserving object, was a reality in the
days of Queen Anne ? Fifty guineas is a somewhat heavy
charge for the pocket ; however, perhaps, Lord Bolingbroke
had come specially provided, or he had a secretary handy who
did not mind the bulging of his coat.

Of this great tragedy, which turned the head of London, and
which the two great political parties vied with each other in
applauding, there are but a few lines virtually existing nowadays. To be sure, it is in print with the rest of Addison's

works, to be read by whosoever will; but very few avail themselves of that privilege.

> 'T is not in mortals to command success.
> But we 'll do more, Sempronius; we 'll deserve it

is the chief relic, and that of a very prosaic common sense and familiar kind, which the great tragedy has left us. "Plato, thou reasonest well!" is another quotation, which is, perhaps, more frequently used in a jocular than serious sense. But for these scraps *Cato* is as dead as most of his contemporaries; and we do not even remember the great tragedy when we hear the name of its author. We think, indeed, only of the "Spectator" if we have read a little in the literature of the period; but if we have no special tastes and studies that way, of Sir Roger de Coverley alone; for Sir Roger is Addison's gift to his country and the world, the creation by which his name will always be known.

The end of a man's life is seldom so interesting as its beginning. After he has achieved all of which he is capable, our interest is more usually a sad than a cheerful one. Addison made in 1716 what seems to have been an ambitious marriage, though he was not the man, one would think, to care for the rank which gave his wife always a distinct personality and another name than his. The Countess of Warwick, however, was, it would appear, a beautiful woman. She had the charge of a troublesome boy, for whom, no doubt, she would be eager to have the advice of such a man as Mr. Addison, whom all the world respected and admired. The little house at Chelsea (the house was called Sandford Manor House, and was some years ago figured against its present doleful background of gasometers, in the *Century*) which that statesman had acquired, and where he delighted to withdraw from the noise and contention of town, was within reach through the fields of Holland House, the

residence of Lady Warwick. They had known each other
for years, and Addison had written exquisite little letters to
the boy-earl — no doubt with intentions upon the heart of
the mother, to which, as is well known, that method is a
very successful way — long before. It was, Dr. Johnson says,
a long and anxious courtship; and perhaps — who knows?
— when Steele performed that picture of the beloved knight
sitting silent before the two fine ladies and unable to articulate
the desires of his honest heart, it was some similar performance
of the shy man of genius who found utterance with such difficulty, which was in Dick's mind. But perhaps Addison grew
bolder when he was a secretary of state. The great Mr. Addison, the delightful " Spectator," the author of " Cato," the man
whose praises were in everybody's mouth, and whom Whig and
Tory delighted to honor, was no insignificant fine gentleman for
a lady of rank to stoop to ; and finally those evening walks over
the fields, and pleasant rural encounters — for Chelsea was the
country in those days, and Holland House quite retired among
all the songsters of the grove, and out of town — came to a
legitimate conclusion. Addison was forty, and her ladyship had
been a widow for fifteen years ; but there is no reason for concluding that there was no romance in the wedding, which, however, is always a nervous sort of business under such circumstances. There was the boy, too, to be taken into account, who
evidently was not a nice boy, but a tale-bearer, who did not
love his mother's faithful lover, and made mischief when he
could. There seems no evidence, however, that the marriage
was unhappy, beyond a malicious note of Pope's, which all the
commentators have enlarged. The poor women who have
the misfortune to be married to men of genius, fare badly at
the hands of the critics. There seems no warrant whatever
for Thackeray's picture of the vulgar vixen whom he calls Mrs.
Steele. Steele's letters exist, but not those of poor Prue, who

was so sadly tried in her husband; and so that suffering woman had to suffer over again in her reputation after her life's trouble is over. It is very unfair to the poor women who have left no champions behind.

The end of our "Spectator's" life was, however, clouded with more than one unfortunate quarrel, the greatest of which has left its sting behind to quiver in Addison's name as long as Pope and he are known. It is neither necessary nor edifying to enter at length into the bitternesses of the past. Pope fancied himself aggrieved in various ways by the man who had warmly acknowledged his youthful merits, and received him (though so much his senior in years and fame) on a footing of equality, and who all through never spoke an ill-natured word of the waspish little poet. He believed, or persuaded himself to believe, in his malignant little soul that Addison was jealous of his greatness, and had set up Tickell to rival him in the translation of Homer; and he believed, or pretended to believe, on the supposed authority of young Warwick, that Addison had hired a vulgar critic to attack him. There seems not the slightest reason to believe that either of these grievances was real. Tickell had written simultaneously a translation, which Addison had read and corrected, on account of which he courteously declined to read Pope's translation of the same, telling him the reason, but accepting the office of critic to the second part of Pope's work. He had himself, according to the poet's brag, accepted Pope's corrections of "Cato," leaving "not a word unchanged that I objected to"; and he was not moved to any retaliation by Pope's attack upon him, but continued serenely to praise his envious little assailant with a magnanimity which is wonderful if he had seen the brilliant and pitiless picture so cunningly drawn within the lines of nature, with every feature travestied so near the real, that even Addison's most faithful partizan has to pause with alarm lest the wicked thing so near the truth might perhaps be true. We hesitate to add to the serene and gentle story of our man of letters this embittered utterance of spite and malice and genius. The lines are sufficiently well known.

Addison did not end his periodical work with the "Spectator." He took up that familiar character once again for a short time, long enough to produce an additional volume,— the eighth,— in which he had no longer the help of his old vivacious companion. The series is full of fine things, but we are not sure, though Macaulay thinks otherwise, that we do not a little miss the light and shade which Steele helped to supply. And other publications followed. Steele himself set up the "Guardian," in which Addison had little share; and various others after that in which he had no share at all. And Addison himself had a "Freeholder," in which he said some notable things; but these are all dead and gone, like so much of the contemporary furnishings of the age. Students find and read them in the old, collected editions; but life and recollection have gone out of them. Perhaps his own time even had by then got as much as it could enjoy and digest out of Addison. We, at least, have done so after these hundred and fifty years, and are capable of no more.

He died in 1719, at the early age of forty-seven. The story goes that he sent for young Warwick when he was on his death-bed, that he might see how a Christian could die: which we should say was unlike Addison, save for the reason that he had been drawing morals all his life, and might at that supreme moment be beyond seeing the ridicule of a last exhibition. Perhaps it was in reality a message of charity and forgiveness to the wayward boy, who, there seems reason to believe, was not fond of his stepfather. And thus the great writer glided gently out of a life in which he had more honor than falls to the lot of most men, and, let us hope, a great deal of mild satisfaction and pleasure. Thackeray has a little scoff at him as a man without passion. "I doubt until after his marriage whether he ever lost his night's rest or his day's tranquillity about any woman in his life." Neither, perhaps, did Sir Roger, whose forty years' love-making and unrequited affection was a sentimental luxury of the most delicate kind, as his maker intended it to be. But Addison's fine and meditative genius had no need of passion. He is the " Spectator " of humankind. He had little temptation in his own calm nature to descend into the arena; the honors of the fight came to him somehow without any soil of the actual engagement. No smoke of gunpowder is about his laurels, no spot of blood upon his sword. He looks on at the others fighting, always with a nod of encouragement for the man of honor and virtue, of keen scorn for the selfish and evil-minded, of pity for the fallen. But it is not his part to fight. He makes no pretense of any inclination that way. He is the looker-on ; and, as such, more valuable than a thousand men-at-arms.

He died at Holland House, that fine historical mansion sacred to the wits of a later age, but which in Addison's time contained no tyrannical tribunal of literary patronage, whatever else there might be there which was contrary to peace. His life and death there make an association more touching, and at the same time of sweeter meaning, than the after-struggles of the Whig men of letters for Lady Holland's arbitrary favors. The great humorist died in the middle of summer, in June, 1719, and was carried from that leafy retirement to the Jerusalem Chamber, where he lay in state : why, it seems difficult to understand — but his position had in it a kind of gentle royalty unlike that of other men. He was buried at Westminster by night, the wonderful solemn arches over the funeral party, half seen by the wavering lights, going off into vistas of mysterious gloom, echoing with the hymns of the choir, who sang him to his rest. Did they sing, one wonders, one of those

verses which had been the most intimate utterance of his life:
that great hymn of creation, scarcely inferior to the angelic mur-
murings of medieval Francis in his cell at Assisi?—

> Soon as the evening shades prevail
> The moon takes up the wondrous tale,
> And nightly to the listening earth
> Repeats the story of her birth;
> Whilst all the stars that round her burn,
> And all the planets in their turn,
> Confirm the tidings as they roll,
> And spread the truth from pole to pole.

Or one of those humble and more fervent human utterances of
faith and humility and thanksgiving?—

> Through every period of my life,
>   Thy goodness I 'll pursue,
> And after death, in distant worlds,
>   The glorious theme renew.
>
> When nature fails, and day and night
>   Divide thy works no more,
> My ever-grateful heart, O Lord,
>   Thy mercy shall adore.
>
> Through all eternity to thee
>   A joyful song I 'll raise,
> But, oh! eternity 's too short
>   To utter all thy praise.

With such a soft, yet rapturous, strain the lofty arches and
half-seen aisles, perhaps with a summer moon looking in, taking
up the wondrous tale, might have echoed over Addison—the
gentlest soul of all those noble comrades who lie together await-
ing the restitution of all things — when our great humorist, our
mildest kind "Spectator," all his comments over, was laid in the
best resting-place England can give to those whom she loves.